BRIGHT
LIGHT
DARK
PANDEMIC

HOW TO ILLUMINATE THE NEED FOR CHANGE MANAGEMENT

By Alejandro Esch

" Leaders today are dealing with not only the pandemic, but the impact of systemic racism, economic instability, the social justice movement, political divisiveness, climate challenges and the intersectionality of all of these issues on employees and business systems. In his new book, *Bright Light Dark Pandemic*, Alejandro D. Esch reminds us how change management principles and practices can guide us through this challenging time. A must read for those who care about their organizations and the people they lead."
--- **Marilyn Nagel, CEO of Diversity Consulting Company, Ready-Aim-Aspire**

"The mix of a change management with a personal account makes for a great read about a challenging topic. It's clear that the learnings from this can be applied to any organization (big or small) wanting to institute a change. I hope that leaders of organizations and countries can put existing biases aside and follow some of these change management principles to guide their people in the future."
--- **Mike Lee, Chief Operating Officer at Two Brain Business, Co-Owner at CrossFit Hale**

"Change is hard. In business it can be difficult for employees to accept change. This may partially be due to a lack of developing and implementing a change management plan. The consequence of a weak to no change management plan in business may equate to a process that is not adopted, low morale or employees leaving. However this is unlike the ultimate consequence of losing human lives as we have witnessed with the pandemic. Bright Light, Dark Pandemic provides an analysis of how the author's change management methodology, "Stop, Prepare, Act," could be applied to how a nation can stop and create urgency in order to prepare its' citizens and implement (act on) a change management strategy. The author provides a chronological review of the steps taken by varied countries in their response to the pandemic. Factual data is presented, along with the author's introspective view of the response that many of us can relate to. It's an engaging read that will cause you to analyze your nation's response, as well as your own, to the pandemic. --- **Rachel Bergman, Vice President at (Fortune 500) Financial Institution**

"...he uses the lens of change management theory to analyze how world governments and the public handled the first months of the pandemic. Through storytelling and anecdotes drawn from analyzing the news, social media, and his life in Costa Rica, Alex pulls you into the confusion and chaos of trying to understand organizational thinking during this crisis. This book outlines a change management theory to critically compare and analyze how government leaders handled the evolving pandemic. More than a sweeping generalization, the analysis focuses on the responses of Costa Rica compared with the United States, in general, and Michigan, his former home state. To add more global perspective, the analysis includes counterpoints from the global perspective of European vs. Asian vs. Central American responses to the data about the virus and human reactions. --- **Steven J. McGriff, Ph.D. DivergentED Consultants**

"The combination of personal stories, events-details, government responses and change management practices make this book unique, in a way that any of us can understand and make ours. Read it, enjoy it, relate to it and its experiences while learning about change management, my passion." ---**Valeria Venegas, Consultant | Professor @ITBA | Partner @Cocolab | PhD Candidate**

"It was a very moving read. I like the approach of the month to month, and even sometimes, day to day tracking of news and activities happening worldwide. It was good to see and hear the view of someone's opinion on the pandemic but even more exciting to visualize it through a worldwide/global lens. The use of change management and continuous improvement/lessons learned was a powerful approach to drill down to the root cause and create the most effective plan to migrate it. --- **Karl Taylor, Inspirational Agile Coach | Servant Leader | Facilitator | Business Agility**

Alejandro Esch provides a historical account of the pandemic and applies it within the context of a change management framework. Providing insights from on the ground in Costa Rica which are juxtaposed against the global response, he makes a compelling argument for the importance of strong leadership, communicating the truth and preparing people for impending change." --- **Daniel Lohr, Director, Localintel**

Copyright

Bright Light Dark Pandemic
Copyright © 2020 Alejandro D. Esch

Printed in the United States of America and Costa Rica

First Printing, 2020

For information contact:
Alejandro Esch
https//www.proactiveperformanceconsulting.com

Cover Design: George Stevens
Editor: Marilyn Alan
Editor: Barbara Esch
Narrator: Bryan Michael

ISBN Print 978-9968-49-568-4
ISBN eBook 978-9968-49-569-1
First Edition, 2020

Dedication

I dedicate this book to all the leaders in the world that supported science, then economy. To all the first responders, medical assistants, doctors, and nurses that have saved so many lives. To the grocery store workers, garbage collectors, delivery people, and all essential needs workers who have risked their lives for us. To all the scientists working on vaccines and treatments. To the private and public sector that have redirected their efforts to work together to help others. To mother nature for slowing us down and giving us a different perspective on life.

Table of Contents

Preface

I tried to calm my anxiety by watching Netflix but became bored after a while. The bombardment of memes wasn't helping either. I remember reading a meme that said, "2020, written by Stephen King and directed by Quentin Tarantino." It was kind of funny to me, but, then again, I was laughing at anything that would temporarily take my mind off reality. I prayed that this pandemic would never happen to humanity again. I know, of course, that a future pandemic is likely, but I hope next time we will be better prepared for it.

I started writing this book as a documentary of how 2020 unraveled itself in locations where I have loved ones. I reckoned maybe in the future my family would like to know what happened during those first four months of the pandemic. However, my background in Performance Improvement and Change Management made the pandemic's sequence of events more appealing to me. I observed that, although countries, cities, and states around the world had access to the same real-time updates of how aggressive the outbreaks were, they didn't all react to the pandemic in the same effective way.

In fact, some countries responded well to the change, yet others were utterly devasted by it. I asked myself, 'Why?' What were the reasons for success or failure? And what can we learn from those exemplars and non-exemplars? That was when I discovered the intention of this book, an idea that had been germinating in my mind since this whole thing began. My aim was twofold: to capture and document some of the incredible events that took place in the world and my challenging journey during this time period and to demonstrate how outcomes could be positively affected by following Change Management principles.

In this book we will cover my Change Management methodology, which we will use to analyze changes that happened during the pandemic, but you will also practice using examples from your real-life. In addition, we will highlight the 10 most significant performance improvement interventions the Costa Rican government implemented that allowed them to successfully manage the pandemic.

At the end of the day, this book is about leadership-accountability. If you consider yourself an actual leader in this world, I welcome you to reflect on the changes that happened within your own sphere of influence (and those of other leaders) during the first four months of the pandemic and to see a fresh perspective including the positive side-effects because of the pandemic. If you continue to be interested in Change Management, there is also an opportunity at the end of the book to take part in a live virtual workshop.

Introduction

The field of Change Management has several models to prepare organizations in successfully making a change. An organization is unique in both structure and size it can be as small as a single person, or a team or a family, or it can be as big as a large corporation, school district, state or country.

When I began writing this book in April 2020, I was living in a small town in Costa Rica. It was difficult to see the silver lining in anything to do with the pandemic. My family on my mother's side all live in Costa Rica. My family on my father's side all live in the United States, mostly in Michigan. As time went by, I couldn't help but notice (from a change management consultant point of view) how well Costa Rica was responding to the pandemic.

Costa Rica is a small Central American country. It has no army and a population of only 5 million people, yet it reacted to the pandemic with the forethought and prioritization of a world power. Its handling of the crisis was especially intriguing to see once we began witnessing the poor responses by powerful countries such as Italy, Spain, and the US, all with an abundance of experts and resources. Never in my wildest dreams did I think the outbreaks would spiral into such a worldwide maelstrom of governmental responses that were, collectively, uncommon, uneven, and unpredictable.

CHAPTER I

December 2019 – The Old Normal

I was lucky to spend last Christmas and New Year's (2019) with part of my family and friends. I didn't realize it would be the penultimate time I would physically be together with my Costa Rican family (mother, stepfather, sister, niece, nephew). During the holidays, we only mentioned the outbreak as a short topic of conversation. The rest of the time we laughed and discussed trivial things such as New Year's resolutions, plans for 2020 and current events. Some global news events during December 2019 were:

- Shooting in Northern Mexico: On December 2, twenty-two people were killed after a shootout between officials and suspected members of the drug cartel. The shooting took place in Northern Mexico. (CNN)

- Iraq Protests Continue: On December 6, a gunman opened fire, and several vehicles went into the crowd of protestors in Baghdad. The attack killed 12 people and wounded.

another 22. The attackers have not been identified as of late. (CNN)

- In pop culture, according to Eonline.com: Harry Styles broke the internet when he gave fans a peek of the fully nude photos that come along with the LP's vinyl packaging.

Thankfully, we also had good news…actual leaders making positive changes in the world—for example, Prime Minister Jacinda Ardern of New Zealand.

Image 1. Prime Minister of New Zealand

"On December 21, nearly 56,000 guns were handed over during New Zealand amnesty. The semi-automat gun ban was set in place after the Christchurch shooting that left 51 people dead earlier this year. (BBC)." On December 9, Finland elected Sanna Marin as Prime Minister, making her the world's youngest Prime Minister. Marin will be sworn in on December 10. (CNN)

These leaders, including the Chancellor of Germany, Angela Merkel and President of Taiwan, Tsai Ing-wen, were the first few leaders to tackle the pandemic head-on and they have continued leading the change in their respective countries. We will cover some reasons these countries performed well during the pandemic, for now let's reflect on how it all started.

Image 2. Chancellor of Germany and Prime Minister of Finland

CHAPTER II

January – How It Started

As I entered the new year, I caught a cold. For a long time, I thought it was just an awful cold, but it felt different. I wasn't feeling feverish, but I was coughing and I could hear my lungs crackling. It lasted all month and into February, I eventually went to a doctor, who told me it was a lung infection. He prescribed antibiotics and, in 5 days, I felt healthy again.

My illness aside, early January was filled with energy and positivity. But then, I began to notice that there was some coverage of a virus spreading in China. I remember being genuinely surprised to see the stringent measures put in place by China to tackle the outbreak that was being reported in Wuhan. I thought, well it IS China and they have a history dealing with SARS, so there was a chance they were just being overly cautious with this new virus. But, by mid-January, I remember thinking the Chinese government was being too aggressive, with the people in Wuhan. I felt angry. Within a day or two, I read the news that the virus had spread to neighboring countries. By mid to late January, cases popped up in other countries near

China, including Thailand, Japan, South Korea, and Vietnam, but also in countries far from China, including Italy, Iran, and the United States.

01.14.2020
NO HUMAN-TO-HUMAN TRANSMISSION

On January 14, the World Health Organization tweeted, "Preliminary investigations conducted by the Chinese authorities have found no clear evidence of human-to-human transmission of the novel virus (2019-nCoV) identified in #Wuhan." This tweet was despite the entire world watching China battle with the rapid spread of the virus. I recall seeing footage of the Chinese military barricading apartment buildings. The news would show tractors pouring sand and rocks in front of apartment building doors, and these apartment buildings contained hundreds of people. From this aggressive reaction, it begged the question, did the Chinese government know that the virus was spreading via people-to-people interaction? They were publicly saying there was no human-to-human transmission, yet they effectively forced everyone to stay home. There was news footage of people apprehended for walking on the streets and of overcrowded hospitals with hundreds of sick people. It would be the first time that the world would see leaked footage of corpses due to the outbreak.

1.19.2020
THE FIRST CASE IN THE USA

A 35-year-old returnee from Wuhan was the first case diagnosed in the US. On Jan 22, President Trump said, "We have it totally under control. It's one person coming in from China. We have it under control. It's going to be just fine" (CNBC interview). On January 29, the

USA established the White House Coronavirus Task Force, and on January 30, the Trump administration barred entry by most foreign nationals who had recently visited China. Every American traveler that had recently visited China was required to quarantine.

Although officials established the Task Force earlier on, they did not introduce a committee until almost a month later on February 26. Vice President Mike Pence was appointed as the Chair and Dr. Deborah Birx as the Response Coordinator. Many others were also appointed, including Dr. Anthony Fauci, who, to some, had become 'the voice of reason' regarding the virus.

01.20.2020
HUMAN-TO-HUMAN TRANSMISSION

On January 20, the World Health Organization confirmed that there was evidence of "limited human-to-human transmission" of the new virus. By January 23, a little over two months after the first confirmed case, China cut off all flights to and from Wuhan, and all public transportation ceased in Wuhan. According to the Johns Hopkins tracking dashboard, there were 830 cases and 25 deaths in China by January 23. Some experts said China's numbers were dramatically low, due to its downplaying the breakout since the beginning. They calculated there might have been up to 10 times more deaths and cases than what China was (and still is) reporting.

The virus was spreading fast. Some countries, like many of those in Asia, seemed better prepared for the virus, perhaps because of past outbreaks—other countries like Iran, Italy, and Spain seemed blindsided, either vastly underprepared for the challenge, or completely unprepared altogether.

1.31.2020
THE FIRST CASE IN ITALY

Two Chinese tourists in Rome tested positive for the virus, followed by a cluster of cases detected in other cities in northern Italy. That day, I learned that the formation of clusters in an outbreak is critical to track because it is essential to link them to one specific case. Track patient number 1 and whom he or she interacted with and test all of them. It is necessary for the containment of a virus and to avoid mass spread. That same day, the Italian government suspended all flights to and from China; they also officially declared themselves in a state of emergency. The World Health Organization (WHO) would begin to refer to the outbreak as a global public health emergency. I remember thinking "Costa Rica has a lot of Italian and Chinese tourists each year. I wonder if the virus is in the country right now?"

CHAPTER III

Change Management

From a Change Management perspective, there is a process that leaders need to follow when they know a change is coming. The change could be a new technology, a new baby, a merger, a market crash, and yes, even a pandemic. Before the change hits them, leaders must determine what the potential impact will have on them. They would do this through a process that we call an Impact Assessment. It's an analysis of how the change will affect distinct groups in an organization, such as a household family, a business, a company department, different world industries, population demographics, and many more areas, depending on the organization. We classify the different impacts as:

Low - Change is Minimal
Medium - Change is Moderate
High -Change is Substantial

Once leaders (e.g., CEOs, Managers, City Officials, Heads of Household, Deans, Principals, Teachers, and others) know the severity of the impact on distinct groups within their organization, they should focus on those groups with high and/or medium change potentials. This is done by communicating and familiarizing the change to those who are most affected. Most importantly, leaders need to create urgency about the impending change. Creating urgency is an essential step in order to build momentum and to mobilize the masses or the individual(s) affected.

To understand how Change Management works, consider the analogy of a traffic light.

- **Red:** Means you should make a *complete Stop.*
- **Yellow:** Is a warning that you should *Prepare* to speed up or to slow down.
- **Green:** Is a signal to go or *Act.* But before you enjoy that sweet acceleration, take a second look both ways to make sure your path is actually clear.

From a change management perspective, leaders must accomplish tasks in each traffic light color / phase before proceeding to the next phase. Here are some of those tasks, including some examples.

Phases	Tasks
RED **(Stop)**	Stop everything and create urgency. Alert those who have been identified as medium-to-highly impacted and communicate the severity of the change to them. Communicate *what* the change is, and *why* it will happen. If possible, communicate *when* it will happen. Communicate what is in it for them, the benefits of preparing for the change. For example, more skills, more money, more hospital beds, more ventilators. Communicate the risk or consequences for not preparing. For example, potential termination, economic collapse, increased deaths, overcrowded hospitals.
YELLOW **(Prepare)**	Begin change management meetings. Prepare and communicate a change management strategy for the upcoming change. Communicate what works well, what is not and what are the next steps. Set expectations and provide a deeper understanding of the specifics in preparing for the change. E.g., We will follow new protocols. We will use new equipment, tools or systems. We will require more resources.

	We will need to complete specific training. We will recognize and reward early adapters to the change. Communicate the consequence for those who are not helping with change and provide appropriate responses to their questions to help manage the change. Communicate that we will send out anonymous readiness surveys on how well prepared people think we are for the change.
GREEN (Act)	Continue change management meetings. Begin implementing change management strategy. For example, Begin and Complete Training program. Begin implementing incentive program to help make the change stick. Begin hiring resources. Begin placing supply orders. Begin sending out change management readiness surveys. Consistently communicate all change management task updates to all impacted (high-medium AND low).

The RED, YELLOW, and GREEN phases build off each other. They're sequential. For example, we cannot skip the red phase (stop) and go straight to the green phase (act). Why not? Because there is a lack of detailed communication about how the change will be managed. People may not feel confident about the organization's preparation for the change and this, in turn, puts at risk their potential support for the change. For example, employees may not have been required to complete trainings to support the change and thus feel unprepared. Maybe they were never directed on how many required resources to hire or the amount and types of supplies to order. Often, leaders drop the ball in some of these phases and tasks and assume people will know what to do. When that happens, it's up to the Change Management consultants to find a remedy.

During the first four months of the pandemic, I thought a lot about Change Management and what phases or tasks leaders may have skipped. As a Change Management consultant, I considered several questions that seemed relevant to each phase:

Phases	Considerations
RED (Stop)	Were the leaders leading the change or downplaying it? Did they create a sense of urgency? Were those that were medium and highly impacted by the change warned? E.g., 1st responders, the elderly, the healthcare industry, transportation industry. Were they informed as to how and why they were identified as moderate-to-highly impacted?

	Did they receive information about what the change was and when it was most likely going to happen? Did they know and understand the benefits of preparing for the change? Did they know the consequences of not changing?
YELLOW (Prepare)	Were those affected informed about exactly what would change for them? E.g., New policies, equipment, tests, processes, curfews, social distancing etc. Were performance improvement measures in place to support the change? E.g., Hospital capacity, enough resources and equipment? Were they informed about what trainings they would need? E.g., State guidelines, testing, contact tracing, best practices and processes. Did those who were impacted feel that the organization was ready for this change?

GREEN (Act)	Did leaders have consistent change management meetings?
	Did leaders implement the change management strategy? E.g. Communication plan, Training program?
	Did they hire needed resources?
	Did they place supply orders on time?
	Did they send out change management readiness surveys?
	Did they have an incentive program in place? (Consequences and rewards)

These are urgent questions that leaders need to answer. Even if leaders do not know all the answers, we should consistently ask them and help leaders find answers. Consistent communication to and by leadership is a must. This will address critical needs, including to help identify red flags, to address frequently asked questions, to prioritize high, mid and low areas of impact, to force decision making, and to communicate solutions. Why is this point so important to underscore? Because many leaders in states and countries did not do this during the pandemic, resulting in devastating consequences.

CHAPTER IV

February – Adapting Early

Towards the end of January and into early February, the Costa Rican government started implementing performance improvement interventions to help mitigate the pandemic. I experienced at least ten such interventions in the months of February, March, and April. I have concluded from seeing these interventions in practice that they are the primary reason Costa Rica's cases and deaths remained low. They are also the reason the Costa Rican hospitals did not overflow with patients and our communities stayed somewhat healthy, which allowed us to open the economy safely.

Let's look at these ten interventions, as they occurred during the following weeks and months.

1st C.R. INTERVENTION: SECURE AIRPORTS

Throughout February, Costa Rica had not had a confirmed case. Nevertheless, airports activated protocols to attend to sick travelers. If a traveler presented with virus symptoms (fever, cough, shortness of breath), pilots or flight attendants communicated with airport health officials, who could then activate the protocol. They would escort the passenger(s) to the ground level, where medical professionals could give tests. Over 150 people were tested at the airport in February. The president also communicated that it was just a matter of time before there would be a case in Costa Rica; indeed, the virus could be here already. To help prevent the spread, the government sent out the World Health Organization (WHO) guidelines for the public via text message and through the news:

- Wash your hands frequently.
- Maintain at least 3 feet away from anyone who is coughing or sneezing.
- Avoid touching your eyes, nose, or mouth; practice good respiratory hygiene.
- If you have a fever, cough, and difficulty breathing, seek medical care early.
- Stay at home if you feel unwell.

The government was preparing for the outbreak and was already creating a sense of urgency that the change was coming and that we would need to make adjustments in our daily lives. Surprisingly, the response of the US leadership was in stark contrast to that of Costa Rica.

THE LOST MONTH

During the entire month of February, President Trump continued to assert that everything in the US was under control. This was despite evidence and warnings from China, Italy, Iran, North Korea, and many more countries who were already grappling with the problem. Trump repeatedly downplayed the severity of the pandemic:

- February 10: "you know in April, supposedly it dies with the hotter weather. — FOX Business.

- February 14: "There's a theory that in April, when it gets warm — historically, that has been able to kill the virus. So, we don't know yet; we're not sure yet. But that's around the corner." — Trump in speaking to National border Patrol Council members.
- February 23: "We have it very much under control in this country." — Trump in speaking to reporters.
- February 26: "And again, when you have 15 people, and the 15 within a couple of days is going to be down to close to zero, that's pretty good job we've done." — Trump at a WhiteHouse Task Force briefing.

According to the Johns Hopkins Virus Resources Center, by February 26 there were 60 cases in the US, only one month after the first case had been identified. One of these was attributed to "community spread," which means it wasn't clear how the patient contracted the virus, because there wasn't a history of the person traveling to any hotspot or having had contact with another person already infected. At this point in time, the US appeared to have no idea how many cases they had. The virus was rapidly spreading out of control. I believe this should have been the red flag for a nationalwide lockdown, in terms of considering needed changes in policy, strategies, and tactics to contain the spread.

On February 26, during a presidential press conference, President Trump was asked if he was worried about the spread of the novel virus in the United States. His reply: "No, because we're ready for it." Reporters then asked if he was considering imposing travel restrictions to and from countries dealing with the outbreak, to which he responded "I may take this step, but right now, it's not the right time."

The next day, February 27, during a meeting with African American leaders, President Trump said: "It's going to disappear. One day — it's like a miracle — it will disappear." He ignored what the epidemiology experts were saying. He downplayed what his own expert, Dr. Anthony Fauci, was telling the public. He ignored visible outbreaks around the world and in his own country. These were only part of a series of unproductive decisions he made as a leader during the early stages of the pandemic in the US, which would prove to have severe consequences in the months to come.

On February 29, the US reported its first death in Washington state. But it turned out not to be the first; it was subsequently discovered that, on February 6, there was an earlier virus death in Santa Clara, California. We can only wonder how different the outcomes might have been had there been an effective response by US officials to identify and implement a system for early detection and treatment.

CHAPTER V

February – Personal Log

On February 7, I realized the sad reality that the world had been maddeningly close to being able to avoid this pandemic in the first place. A headline on the BBC read: "Li Wenliang: virus kills Chinese whistleblower." I dug in a little more and, according to Wikipedia, in late December 2019, Dr. Li Wenliang was one of eight other doctors warning people of a human-to-human outbreak of what they thought was SARS. On January 3, Dr. Li was summoned to the Wuhan Public Security Bureau and told to sign an official confession letter promising to cease spreading false "rumors" regarding the virus. In the letter, he was rebuked for making malicious comments by announcing seven cases of SARS at the Huanan

Seafood Wholesale Market. It had "severely disturbed the social order."

Again, according to Wikipedia, the letter stated, "We solemnly warn you: If you keep being stubborn, with such impertinence, and continue this illegal activity, you will be brought to justice—is that understood?" Li signed the confession writing: "Yes, I understand." The implication, of course, was that his life may have been in danger if he did not sign the confession.

On January 28, China's Supreme Court apologized by writing a message on its official WeChat account saying, "they should not have been punished as what they said was not entirely false." On January 30, almost a month after Dr. Li warned of the probability of human-to-human transmission, the World Health Organization declared the virus a public health emergency. A week later, Dr. Li died due to the virus.

Dr. Li and the seven other doctors showed incredible bravery in trying to limit, contain, or stop the outbreak altogether. A study from the University of Southampton suggests that if the Chinese government had listened to Dr. Li initially, the number of cases could have reduced as much as 95%. The virus would have been contained. These doctors dared to speak out, at the risk of being suppressed, censored, or worse, arrested and even killed. We can only hope that they and their bravery live long in our memories and serve as exemplars for us all.

CHAPTER VI

March – A Sense of Urgency

March was the month when the pandemic became real to me. For starters, Costa Rica identified its first two suspected cases. These two cases rocked us with fear, because we had seen footage coming out of Italy and Spain and it was tragic. In the back of our minds, we knew that Latin America resembles these European countries, in terms of cultural practices that include being politically disorganized, vast families living together, kissing when we see each other, group and family gatherings. We knew that this "culture" was one of the primary causes for such a fast spread of the virus in Italy and Spain. I remember thinking it would quickly wipe us out if it came to Costa Rica.

On February 29, two Costa Rican ladies returned home from a trip to Italy. Once home, they reported not feeling well. Ironically, one is a doctor who works for the Ministry of Health in Costa Rica, so she contacted her colleagues to get herself and her travel companion tested. The news that they were being tested spread quickly. The threat seemed real and it shocked us all. For me, it was particularly scary because I happen to know both of these ladies. I see them frequently at family events, as they're aunts of my girlfriend. One of them lives only three miles from my house. This, indeed, was close to home for me (literally). Officials moved the aunts to the Costa Rican Institute of Research and both were tested twice. The country was quietly awaiting their test results. My girlfriend and I were in constant worry that they would get sick, but we were also in regular communication with them and they assured us they were fine. Within 24 hours, all tests came back negative. It was a false alarm; Costa Rica could breathe again. We were so happy! However, five days later, on March 6, bad news arrived. A tourist from New York had been traveling all over Costa Rica for a week had tested positive. Once again, Costa Rica was in shock.

Three days after that, March 10, the first person in Michigan tested positive, and I worried about my parents living there. On March 1, actor Tom Hanks and his wife, Rita Wilson, tweeted that they both had contracted the virus. This was the first time I realized that nobody was immune to this virus. Money, fame, or familiarity would not help. On this day, the World Health Organization formally declared it a Pandemic.

In Costa Rica, the cases rapidly increased to 13, including a 2-year-old baby. On March 11, there were 22 cases in the country and, by March 15, we had 37 infected. It was incredible how fast the numbers were rising. All I could think about was the desperate footage of the hospitals in Italy.

2ND C.R. INTERVENTION: LISTEN TO EXPERTS

Image 5. Dr. Daniel Salas

The first time I remember paying attention to Dr. Daniel Salas was when the cases reached 54 in just four days. The entire country was watching him. He was looking at the camera with the most intense conviction. I had never seen someone that serious and passionate in my life. I felt like we were about to go to war, and he was talking to me directly. He was almost tearing up from emotion when he said Costa Rica now had 54 confirmed cases. My heart dropped. He immediately told us, this is "not a joke" and to not take it lightly. His conviction and direction on what to do and what to expect had perfect timing. It was right before people started to panic; which in my opinion helped many avoid the feeling of hopelessness. He assured us there was no reason to fear; we have enough resources for months to come; we only need to follow the day-to-day rules. In other words, he *Stopped* us (Red Phase), communicated the change and created urgency, he also *Prepared* us (Yellow Phase), communicated the situation, set expectations and let us know the benefits and consequences of the change, which motivated us to change.

26

I remember him saying that the number of cases would, indeed, go up, there would be no way around that. But, then the cases would plateau and go down. He challenged each of us to decide how high or low we wanted the numbers to go, by our collective actions. How many deaths do we want in our country? He said these deaths could be anybody...grandma, mother, brother, sister, no matter what age. Anybody! That even movie stars get it, kings, children, poor, rich, black, white, it doesn't matter. He also reminded us of Italy and Spain and what happened to them for not preparing and not behaving accordingly.

Dr. Salas and the Costa Rican government had a plan which they communicated and *Acted* on (Green Phase). Dr. Salas has the same conviction now as the first day I heard him. As conspiracy theories increased around the world, he would consistently debunk them with full transparency. As a result, most people are still listening to him. Without a doubt in my mind, Daniel Salas, President of Social Security Roman Macaya and the President of Costa Rica, Carlos Alvarado, are a huge reason we didn't end up like Italy. Of course, first responders, police, grocery store clerks, and many more are the true heroes. I would like to share with you a quote from Daniel Salas, whom I consider a great leader: "STAY AT HOME!"

3ᴿᴰ C.R. INTERVENTION: CONTROL CROWDS

The government immediately rolled out street billboards as well as text messages sent to our cell phones and commercials on TV, all providing reminders to wash our hands and to practice social distancing. By March 15, only five days after the first case, Costa Rica closed all bars, beaches, and national parks. Restaurants could only stay open with a maximum of 50% capacity. By March 16, the MEP (Ministry of Public Schools) had closed all public schools, and private schools followed a week later. On March 17, the popular national soccer tournament canceled its activities. By March 18, Costa Rica closed its borders to foreigners and non-residents, and on March 19, the government enforced a mandatory 14-day quarantine for all civilians.

Starting March 24, there was a nationwide vehicle restriction between the hours of 10 p.m. and 5 a.m. Most vehicles were restricted on Costa Rica's roads between those nighttime hours with a list of exceptions, which included:

- Transport of cargo/merchandise.
- Public transportation, including buses and taxis. Buses needed to have every other seat empty and no one was allowed to stand.
- Vehicles making home delivery of food, medications, and other essentials.
- People driving to/from work corresponding to those nighttime hours.
- Trash collection and construction vehicles.
- Official law enforcement vehicles and ambulances.
- Those driving to a hospital or pharmacy for a health emergency.

COSTA RICA'S EPICENTER

The epicenter started in a county called Alajuela, beginning with a doctor who was unaware he had the disease, and, thus, was unknowingly infecting dozens of people. Within a month, he had died. The second most infected county at the time was San Jose, the capital of Costa Rica. Within a month, it had become the new epicenter. I had particular concerns about this shift, because my mother and stepfather live in San Jose, both in their 70s and both with serious lung issues. An impoverished area called Desamparados had the third highest infection rates, and the wealthiest county in Costa Rica, Santa Ana, reported the fourth highest number of cases.

In March, cases were increasing by about 20 per day. We knew it would only get worse. The stress was building up. The dampening effects on social gatherings were beginning to be seen everywhere. On

March 9, the famous South-by-Southwest (SXSW) Festival in Austin, Texas was canceled for the first time in 38 years. I had a flight already booked to Austin for early April to meet my parents for a long weekend and to attend a conference together. Despite the cancelation of SXSW, my parents and I were tentatively keeping our plans in place at that time. However, cases started escalating in the States and, on March 10, Michigan (where my parents live), saw its first case, the beginning of a spread that would eventually make it the fourth most infected state in the US. As cases increased in the US, the Austin conference we were going to attend moved virtual. Also, there was a lot of talk about the virus affecting older people the most; later, of course, we learned that all age groups were reporting infections; no single demographic seemed to be exempt. At this point, we decided to cancel our trip, a disappointment for sure, but in retrospect it was the right call because things became much worse very fast.

4TH C.R. INTERVENTION: ALTER SHOPPING

From a change management point of view, I was encouraged and impressed to see that the Costa Rican government had the foresight to quickly address the spread by putting several measures in place in the marketplace. Almost overnight, we noticed there were limits on the number of people allowed in grocery stores, the number of items each person could buy (thus reducing their time in the store) and tape markers appeared on store floors, effectively keeping people physically distanced while they were waiting in lines.

In retrospect, these were smart and quick governmental decisions that prevented, or at least significantly mitigated, more negative consequences down the road. Without such leadership and policy guidelines, it's not unreasonable to assume that people would have continued to behave the way they had in pre-pandemic days, by habit, but with the effect of those behaviors now being seen as socially irresponsible. On March 23, plastic barriers were mandated at store checkouts, to protect cashiers and customers alike. These decisions prevented food and cleaning products from running out, which, in turn, allowed more of these essentials to be dispersed evenly across the community. It also reduced the spread of the virus across the board.

IN OTHER GLOBAL NEWS

On March 1, New York City identified its first case, a woman traveling back from Iran. (Note: It shouldn't be assumed, however, that this was the virus's path to the US; experts suspect that the first case in the US most likely came from Europe).

In trying to understand leaders' actions or the lack thereof, some countries present compelling lessons for us. In March, the four highest rate countries were China, South Korea, Italy, and Iran, in that order. It's hard to know why these countries experienced such high case rates, but it's possible that, among them, preserving their economic interrelationships was seen by leaders as a bigger threat to their respective countries than the one that presented to their citizen's health.

Certainly, there was failure to create a sense of urgency and to prepare for a virus outbreak that many knew was coming. Iran, for example, during this crucial time did not adequately familiarize or prepare its citizens, instead blaming outside actors, including the West. On March 7 according to the LA Times, Iranian President Hassan Rouhani said, "Iran's enemies are trying to create panic about the virus to shut down society." Assigning blame is unproductive in the face of a dire threat like a virus, though. It delays taking effective action and signals to citizens that behaving status quo is appropriate. In fact, just a week earlier in late February, the deputy health minister and head of Iran's counter virus task force, Iraj Harirchi, downplayed the outbreak on national television. All was not well, though. During the broadcast, he appeared pale, using tissue paper to wipe his face, and, a day later, it was reported that he had tested positive for the virus. The result, however difficult for Harirchi, was that he changed his opinion about the virus and behavioral changes began to occur in Iran. More people started social distancing and Iran began to see a decrease in infections.

According to the Johns Hopkins virus tracker, by mid-April, Iran went from fourth to eighth in number of cases in the world.

The second most infected country at the time was South Korea, between China and Italy in incidence rates. On Feb 24, according to the New York Times, Korean news was calling the pandemic the "Moon Jae-in Virus." Moon Jae-in is the president of South Korea, who was seen to be downplaying the virus. China is South Korea's largest trading partner, and the lack of an urgent response by South Korea was attributed, by many, to the country's ties with China. Some accused Moon of failing to protect public health due to fears that closing the borders would displease the Chinese government, in contrast to Taiwan and Hong Kong's aggressive reaction to the virus that started in January. Both of those countries had already closed their borders to China for over a month. By March, Taiwan had only 49 cases confirmed and one death and Hong Kong reported 100 cases and 2 deaths. By contrast, South Korea had already reported 5,766 cases and 35 deaths.

It was speculated that this quick spike in South Korea's cases was related to an eccentric religious group called the Shincheonji Church of Jesus, based in Daegu. According to the BBC, more than half of South Korea's cases were either centered in or related to members of this church who would congregate in secret, taking part in large group ceremonies, sometimes hundreds at a time. The government eventually dismantled these mass gatherings, which no doubt helped flatten the curve. That said, South Korea also had more testing capability than most other countries, so logically they could report more cases.

Italy, also, found it challenging to prepare its citizens for behavioral changes that were needed to mitigate the pandemic. Even with several cases already identified in the country, the governmental response was to downplay the threat. According to QRIUS.com, from the outset, Italy's government miscommunicated the severity of the pandemic, with little transparency and repeated hesitations by officials. Politicians, and even some scientists, claimed that the virus was nothing more than ordinary seasonal flu. They even asked for events, exhibitions, and sports matches to proceed, citing economic reasons. Similar to other countries, the economy undoubtedly played a role in pandemic-related decision making on the part of leaders. Northern Italy (where the outbreak started) has a large fashion industry that has direct economic ties to China, so it was not in their best economic interest to prohibit flights coming in from China.

It's also been speculated that the hard spike in Italy was related to their cultural practices. Hugging and kissing each other to say hello, multigenerational families with grandma and grandpa all living in the same house; these would become factors in the rise of cases, along with the number of older people in the population. For example, 23% of Italy's population was over 65, a high percentage compared to that of other European countries.

Image 6. Italian Flag

According to the Johns Hopkins virus tracker, by March 7, Italy had reported a jaw-dropping 1247 new cases and 36 deaths in one day; a total of 5,884 cases and 233 deaths. The numbers were unheard of at the time. News during March showed Italy's death toll increasing dramatically, pictures of corpses, mass graves, desperate doctors and nurses pleading for resources, and videos of overcrowded hospitals. It was so devastating that medical students were pulled out of schools and immediately put into hospitals to help. Doctors from other countries such as Albania came to provide support.

Image 7. Albanians Doctors helping Italy

Seeing the televised daily news in Costa Rica about what was happening in Italy and Spain was like watching a live war every day. It was incredibly sad. By early April, Italy would report an astounding 136,000 cases and 17,000 deaths.

03.14.2020
NICARAGUA HAS LOVE FESTIVAL

Here in Central America, Nicaragua, our neighboring country to the north, didn't seem to be responding in any positive way to the danger of the virus. In fact, some actions seemed completely counter-intuitive. On March 14, there was a "love fest" with hundreds of people marching to beat the virus with the 'power of love'. On April 6, there was a summer carnival with four thousand people attending. In fact, throughout this pandemic, Nicaragua has appeared to enthusiastically encourage tourism, soccer games, and national sports. Life was going on like everything was normal there. Concerts, parties, festivals, and churches…all filled with people. How could it be that they had only reported two cases and zero deaths? When I heard this, the first thing that came to mind was that this was a ticking time bomb. Nicaragua is

33

the poorest country in Central America, headed by a dictator named Daniel Ortega and his wife, Rosario Murillo. With few resources in the country and a lack of leadership to help people avoid contracting the virus, it was just a matter of time before a colossal outbreak happened. Where, I wondered, would all the Nicaraguan people go for healthcare? My guess, Costa Rica.

03.26.2020
USA BECOMES THE GLOBAL EPICENTER

By March 26, the US became the world's hotspot and New York became the epicenter's epicenter. Lack of ventilators, masks, and testing kits were serious concerns in New York and in many other places. Across the US, state governors were pleading with the President to invoke the Defense Production Act, a measure that would compel companies to retool and manufacture these critical items needed to defeat the pandemic. President Trump's response to the governors' requests seemed inexplicit and political. By failing to create a Federal-level mandate that would direct US companies to fill the need for vital equipment, states were left to compete with one another for these urgently needed resources, a situation that effectively created a bidding war between the states.

It sounds crazy, but a day earlier, on March 25, President Trump stated that he wanted to open the US economy by Easter Sunday (April 13) and would like to see churches packed. For us in Costa Rica and probably in most of the world, this statement was utterly irrational. The US was in the midst of their spike in cases and deaths. In fact, the US, with 81,864 reported cases, had officially become the world's most infected nation, surpassing China who had, at that point, reported 81,285 cases. I remember thinking that, if Trump opened the US economy in two weeks, he will have single-handedly sparked the decline, not the rise, of the US economy. By ignoring his experts, the data, and the rise in deaths and spread going on globally (indeed, even in his home state of New York), his action would have prolonged and exacerbated, not contained and reduced, the impact of the pandemic.

By March 25, only 25 days after its first case, New York State had over 4000 cases. A vast amount of cases in a short amount of time. One reason experts believed it spiked so rapidly was due to the amount of foot traffic in New York City, in conjunction with not shutting down soon enough. For example, the non-essential businesses did not close their doors until over 10,000 cases had been confirmed. By contrast, here in Costa Rica, the government had mandated closure of non-essential businesses after just over 100 cases.

On March 30, New York City had reason to hope. A huge floating hospital, the USNS Comfort, arrived in their harbor to help treat the infected, which had grown to more than 30,000. I felt surprise and relief at this government support for the City. And, like many, I felt encouraged at this impressive sight.

Image 8. Rescue Medical Ship in NYC Bay.

CHAPTER VII

March –Personal Log

I remember being excited that March had arrived because it was my birthday month and I was making plans with friends and family. I had booked a flight from Costa Rica to meet up with my parents (dad and stepmom), who would come from Michigan, at a conference in Austin, Texas. I was excited about that because we do not see each other often and we always have a great time together when we do connect.

On March 7, my aunt and cousins, visiting in Costa Rica from Switzerland, generously hosted a lovely family reunion with over 50 people. It was great to have the whole Costa Rican family all in one room, which is not very easy to do. I remember noticing during the reunion that no one was social distancing. Everyone was hugging and kissing. It was great! It would be the last time I would physically touch or see my family for a long time.

This shows some of my family. My aunt and cousins stayed for a couple weeks longer after this picture was taken and then returned to Switzerland, just in time, as it turned out. The day after they left, March 18, the Costa Rican government closed its borders. Switzerland at the time already had reported nearly five thousand cases and 43 deaths. That was a considerable number for such a small country. I worried about my aunt and cousins going home, but they made it safely, and they were surprisingly calm about the whole thing.

By mid-March, the world had transformed. The number of people dying each day in Italy and Spain was jarring. Plus, the cases in the US were rising rapidly. I felt scared, confused, angry, stressed, sad. I felt multiple emotions multiple times a day. My girlfriend and I decided to move in together, just in case one of us got sick. Plus, she lives in a more congested part of town than I do, so it would be safer for her to live with me. The stress went from 1 to 10 very fast all over the country; the panic people felt was rising. Some people bought up what seemed to be the entire grocery store. However, most Costa Ricans waited for our leaders to guide us. They had already shown good leadership and decision-making in handling the pandemic and that went a long way to engender our trust. In the media, the President would come on to set the tone, but most of the nuts and bolts information would come from the Ministry of Health. Every day at 12:30 p.m., the country would stop and listen to the Ministry's head, Daniel Salas, as he updated us and gave guidelines for practical actions that we, as citizens, could take to help promote the safety of everyone in our country.

THE SOCIALLY IRRESPONSIBLE

The brilliant late comedian George Carlin once said, "Never underestimate the power of stupid people in large groups." For sure, large groups tend to foster herd behavior. And, although it's not useful to assign "stupid" labels to people, it's important to understand actions that people choose to do that endanger public safety. Herd behavior can obscure clear thinking, block concern for others, and energize selfishness. Results are not always positive. For example, on March 15, Costa Rica called for the closure of all bars, beaches, and national parks. On March 16, the Ministry of Public Schools shut down the schools. Trying to get in one last vacation, hundreds of young people and families flocked to the beaches. On March 19, in an effort to get people to return home, the government installed a mandatory 14-day stay-at-home quarantine. However, it took some time to get people off the beaches, especially the surfers. Police arrested the national champion surfer who was surfing; as punishment, he had to pay a fine and issue a public apology, urging people to stay at home.

Other surfers were still breaking the law. The police force shot at one for running away from a cop, causing no small amount of controversy on gun use. Most Costa Ricans seemed to side with the police. Around two weeks after hundreds of people had illegally escaped to the beaches, Costa Rica felt its first spike in cases. By March 29, Costa Rica had reported 314 confirmed cases, 2 deaths, and 3 who had recovered.

Image 9. Surfer running from police

MY FIRST BREAKDOWN

During this time, I recall hearing that, in Italy, mouth-to-mouth resuscitation was prohibited because doctors were contracting the virus. Doctors had to decide who would live and who would die because ventilators were in such critically short supply. It would cross my mind every day that it would be easy for Costa Rica to end up like Italy or Spain (or even worse!) as both countries are more developed. The anxiety was increasing quickly. I recall seeing, for the first time, Italians singing beautiful opera songs on their balconies. They were singing to give each other a little hope as they were in the middle of a warlike pandemic. Seeing this made me stop what I was doing and break down crying. I could not believe what our reality had become.

My girlfriend also had a breakdown because she so worried about her mom and dad, who live four hours away, on the Caribbean coast of Costa Rica. She was really feeling torn loyalties, wanting to be with them in case one of them got sick, but also not wanting to leave me alone in case I got ill. We talked about it one night and mutually decided she was better off with her parents. We reasoned that I had a better chance of surviving the virus than her parents. I also had Rafie, my dog, as company. So, she stayed until my birthday (end of March). I'm glad she did.

On a financial level, I was worried. I am an independent consultant, so I work for myself, and business stopped coming in. A large international nonprofit organization was one of my past clients, and I was planning to continue working for them in 2020. The Costa Rican

Government had partnered with this organization to help increase the number of bilingual people in the country and I had been hired to provide Change Management expertise for this program, which included over 150 volunteers. However, once the Costa Rican borders closed, all the volunteers had to leave the country. The project was frozen and, just like that, I had no significant income.

I took stock of my situation. I have an apartment that I rent out to students, but it was empty at the moment. I needed to get a new tenant and to find a remote job as soon as possible. I knew things were likely to get worse, so I started publicizing the apartment everywhere. I applied for jobs. I continued to assess what I had and where I was at with all of this. One job lead seemed promising; it was as a Spanish-English interpreter, well within my skill set. The interviews were smooth. They offered me the job. All that needed to be done was to sign the contract, but that required me to show up in person. No electronic signatures were allowed. I was scheduled to sign on April 1. However, by late March, the company's offices were closed and all contract signings had been frozen until they could be done in person. This was a blow, because the job had looked so promising. All I could do was to keep looking.

Adding insult to injury, there was a water shortage during this time. Every year during the summer in Costa Rica, there is a shortage of water. This means no water from 10 a.m. to 6 p.m., every other day. At the same time, though, there was also a shortage of rubbing alcohol and gel alcohol. I had gotten used to water shortages in the past, but the outbreak only compounded the challenge; the virus was everywhere. On the doorknob, on my shoes, on my dog's paws, on my glasses, everywhere. Not having water to wash my hands easily was incredibly frustrating. I ended up buying a good-sized water tank and filled it with water, but it was still a pain to shower or to wash things. Thank God the rainy season was coming in a couple of months.

MY 1ST VIRTUAL BIRTHDAY

By this point, I was looking forward to my birthday. My girlfriend was returning to her parents' house soon, and I was determined to have fun. On my birthday, I woke up to the news that Boris Johnson had contracted the virus. Johnson, the Prime Minister of the United Kingdom, was another leader who had downplayed the severity of the pandemic, causing England to lead in European virus deaths, surpassing even Italy. I remember thinking, maybe this personal experience with the virus would change Johnson's mind about the severity of the pandemic. It was encouraging to think a change of mind might result in a change in policy. I could only hope.

Optimism and being "birthday spoiled" was a therapeutic combination. My sweet girlfriend made breakfast that morning. Then, we picked up a birthday cake for our celebration in the evening. During the day, she worked (remotely), while I went out and bought some balloons, meat, veggies, beers, and wine. The grocery store was packed. Luckily, I had under ten items, so I went in the fast lane – in and out quickly – yes! I also remember that all the clerks had a plastic shield between them and the customers. It thrilled me to see that – security – yes again!

I moved fast at the grocery store; it felt like an old video game that I played as a kid called Frogger, where a frog had to cross a street and avoid the cars whizzing by. I had to avoid the other shoppers the same way. In the middle of this real-life game, I must have dropped my squirt bottle with rubbing alcohol. I remember feeling crushed about it; it felt like I lost my cell phone. It's because disinfectant was hard to find at the time. However, I decided to not let it ruin my day and, once I was home, I swung into birthday mode. Nothing would stop me from having a good time.

As I was preparing for the virtual party, I got a call from a guy that had seen the apartment a few days back. He was interested in the apartment and wanted to move in the beginning of April. It was amazing! Best birthday present ever! Birthday evening, my girlfriend had secretly planned a little virtual surprise party with my family. Everyone jumped on Skype, they sang happy birthday to me, and we drank wine, ate, and talked for hours. We shared quarantine

.periences, Netflix shows, and much more. Even though it was virtual, I felt closer to them than ever before. I hoped other families were feeling the same type of love and connections with their loved ones.

On March 29, my girlfriend left for her hometown, Limon, where there was only one reported case at the time. That was reassuring. But, we both felt sad and nervous that day. Sad because we weren't sure when we would see each other again, and nervous because she was taking an Uber there. We cleaned and disinfected the car before she got in. She wore a mask for the entire trip back. Because of the low number of cases in Limon, there were civilians in the city blocking some roads to prevent people from coming in, trying to stave off possible carriers of the virus. Luckily, she left early. It was the right decision – she got through without problems, and her parents were delighted and relieved.

As harsh as March was to us, I remember feeling the irony of it all. I treasured more than ever my contacts with family and friends. And I felt actually grateful that the pandemic happened in the sense that it gave the planet a breather. I had wanted that to happen, to have real Earth Days. With no cars, the air felt cleaner, I could hear more birds in the trees, see and smell more vegetation, and the sky was crystal clear during the night. The news would report beautiful stories like satellite images of the earth rejuvenating, wild animals coming out of the forests, and playing naturally on the beaches. My girlfriend saw a manatee swim up a canal in her hometown. It's incredible what a difference only two months can make on the Earth. I hope we learn from this and take care of our planet more. When all of this is over, it would be great if we adopted a global quarantine month to give our planet a break.

CHAPTER VIII

April – Protocols Enforced

By the end of April, the Costa Rican government had implemented and enforced 10 performance improvement interventions, starting with activating airport protocols, listening to the experts, activating crowd control, and activating store protocols. Let's look at the others.

5TH C.R. INTERVENTION: ACTIVATE LOCAL LEADERSHIP

This intervention was a big ask for the Costa Rican government as local leadership needed to communicate and enforce restrictions. To my surprise, this wasn't happening in other places outside Costa Rica. I know this because one of my best friends lives in Brooklyn, New York. On March 23rd, I asked him how many cases had been reported there. He couldn't answer me. In fact, he replied sarcastically, "Let me yell out the window and ask." He eventually sent me a data dashboard for the entire State of New York, but he didn't know the situation in his own borough. That surprised me because, in Costa Rica from the beginning of March, each county mayor would send out daily dashboard reports with each county's status. The format for reporting was always the same. It showed confirmed cases, new cases, deaths, and total recovered. It also reported discarded tests, total tests, number of men, number of women, age-range, and percentage of cases by county, followed by the actual number of cases for each county.

I know that Costa Rica is a lot smaller than New York, but it's about the population size of a couple of New York's boroughs put together. To me, it seemed like an incredible gap that New York's boroughs failed to communicate to its people on a daily basis the number of cases and fatalities.

I believe if they had done so, it would have helped with flattening the curve. People may have protected themselves and others more with mask-wearing, staying inside, or, at least, they may have felt like the district handled the situation adequately. They may have taken pride in the fact that their collective actions helped reduce the number of cases in their borough. Here in Costa Rica, it became a bit of a badge of honor to have fewer cases than the next county. We didn't want to move up on the list.

A few days later, on March 25, I asked my NYC friend if parks in Brooklyn or New York City had been closed yet. He said that they had not, and that, two days previous, Governor Cuomo had given the city 24 hours to come up with a plan, so far with no result.

6TH C.R. INTERVENTION: IMPLEMENT DRIVING RESTRICTIONS

Why should organizations, including individuals, want to adapt to a Change? What's attractive about the change? What is in it for them? Often, people get on board with changes that need to be made not because of the traditional "plus" benefits in doing so but, rather, as a benefit of avoiding undesired consequences. Avoiding aversiveness works well, in general, but especially for people who may not be highly motivated solely by social responsibility.

Costa Rica grappled with designing effective consequences that would result in change compliance. Many people were not staying home and socially distancing. So, first, officials established day restrictions. Driving on a restricted day meant they would take your license plate off your car and issue a ticket, along with adding six points to your driver's license. Of course, there were exceptions to the law, depending on your job requirements, but, in general, restrictions were strict and they were enforced. I believe that this was one of the key factors in how Costa Rica quickly flattened its curve, at least initially.

On April 1, the government enforced its 2nd driving restriction law from April 3 to Tuesday, April 7. The curfew imposed on driving at night dropped from 10 pm to 5 pm. We could no longer drive after 5 pm, with exceptions depending on your job. But also, they placed a day time restriction depending on your vehicle's license plate:

- Restrictions on Saturday and Monday for plates ending in 0, 2, 4, 6, 8.
- Restrictions on Sunday and Tuesday for plates ending in 1, 3, 5, 7, 9.
  Most commercial businesses must remain closed. Delivery services are still permitted, and essential businesses (including grocery stores and pharmacies) can stay open.
- Limited long-distance public transportation (75 km or farther).

One would think that all these restrictions would have resonated with people who weren't already getting on board, but think again. So, the government added another strict measure, probably because Holy Week was coming up, which is typically a big party week across the whole country. From April 8 to 12, we would now have to observe the vehicle restrictions at all times.

• Wednesday, April 8: Vehicles with license plates ending in **0 and 1** may drive with restrictions to only the supermarkets, pharmacies, and health centers. Other vehicles are banned from public roads.

• Thursday, April 9: Vehicles with license plates ending in **2 and 3** may drive with the same restrictions.

• Friday, April 10: Vehicles with license plates ending in **4 and 5** may drive with the same restrictions.

• Saturday, April 11: Vehicles with license plates ending in **6 and 7** may drive with same restrictions.

• Sunday, April 12: Vehicles with license plates ending in **8 and 9** may drive with the same restrictions. All public transportation, except taxis and some essential routes, was to be suspended. Even with all these restrictions, by April 15, more than 2700 license plates had been confiscated, and that was only in the San Jose metro area!

All this illustrates what a logistical nightmare it is to identify, establish, and enforce effective consequences for groups of people who all have different motivations, feelings of social responsibility, and risk tolerance. Throughout this time, Costa Rican officials monitored how our society was behaving and responded quickly to modify restrictions as needed to ensure the flattest curve possible.

Here is a picture I took by my house of the police stopping people who were breaking curfew or driving illegally.

7ᵀᴴ C.R. INTERVENTION: CONTROL BORDERS

On April 3, while most nations in the world were taking severe measures to prevent mass gatherings, the government of Nicaragua was doing the opposite. The government and the Institute of Tourism (Intur) were promoting and inviting their nation to take part in their yearly Summer Carnival.

Image 11. Daniel Ortega

Nicaragua, at the time, had reported five cases and one death. In Costa Rica, we were hearing about more and more cases coming out of Nicaragua.

On April 10, Nicaragua released 1700 prisoners, ostensibly because of good behavior. Rumors spread that the real reason was because of an outbreak in those prisons. In April, more and more Nicaraguans were coming into Costa Rica. Costa Rica closed its border in mid-March and, by April 11, they had rejected 5,357 foreigners at the border, and most of these people were from Nicaragua. The government sent reinforcements there to help control the 300-kilometer border. On April 13, the Costa Rican government installed an airbase on the CR-Nicaraguan border to reinforce surveillance.

By early May, there were reports that the Nicaraguan government was forcing its citizens to bury their dead at night, without ceremony, to avoid international news coverage.

Image 12. of Makeshift Costa Airport on boarder

Panama, Costa Rica's neighbor to the south, took the opposite approach from Nicaragua to the pandemic. They had a stringent policy with their citizens. They detained people who broke quarantine, jailed them for 24 hours, and required them to subsequently complete 24 hours of community service. The second-time offenders were also arrested for 24 hours but required to do four days of community service. On April 5, Panama confirmed 1,988 cases and 54 deaths.

8ᵀᴴ C.R. INTERVENTION:

INFORM CHILDREN

Image 14. COVID-19 Children's book

April 23 was International Book Day. The Costa Rican government partnered with the United Nations to provide a free, illustrated book to help children understand and come to terms with the pandemic. The title of the book is *Los días que TODO se detuvo* ("The days when EVERYTHING stopped"). A similar book was developed in English by the IASC which was a collaborative effort of over 1700 parents, children, caregivers and teacher around the world sharing how they were coping with the pandemic.

So, why is it important to highlight this as the 8th performance improvement intervention undertaken by the Costa Rican government? It's because children are highly social, especially at school, perhaps even more so than most adults in their daily routines. Children also physically touch many, many things throughout the day, which can potentially spread the virus even more. They also can be asymptomatic, unknowingly spreading the virus to their own families. So, it's critical that they and their parents understand the safety rules of the pandemic. It's also crucial that they know what is going on from an early age, as this may not be the last pandemic they experience.

On April 24, Sesame Street and CNN produced a 90-minute special to answer pandemic questions that they solicited from children around the world. It was a great idea, as children may not have understood how and why life seemed so different all of a sudden. The questions illustrate the breadth of information that children (and others) were seeking:

- Lucy, a 7-year-old from Alexandria, Virginia, and 9-year-old Julian from Kiev, Ukraine, are curious if people can get the virus from the water.

- Abby Cadabby's friend, James, wanted to know what the virus looks like.

- Twins Bryce and Brody, 6, from Sands Point, New York, asked why soap won't kill the virus if you eat it.

- Siblings Lucas and Avery asked, "when will this be over?"

9th C.R. INTERVENTION: OPEN ECONOMY WITH PROTOCOLS

On April 24, Costa Rica reported its lowest number of cases in one day, only one. Cases had been decreasing for weeks. Stats showed 687 cases, six deaths, and 216 recovered, so it seemed that we Costa Ricans had been behaving pretty well, and our efforts had paid off enough to partially reopen the economy.

On April 27, the President informed us of new guidelines:

- Movie theaters will open during the week with separation of seating of 2 meters (6.5 feet)

- Parks will open at 25% capacity to practice non-contact sports, only no gathering or sitting.

- Gyms and swimming pools will open during the workweek with 25% capacity.

- Work offices, services and activity centers will open but must have 2 meters between seats. They must adhere to a long list of prevention protocols.
- Work establishments must promote working from home as a priority.
- Barbershops and salons will open at 50% capacity.
- The same vehicle restrictions are in place until May 15.
- Auto stores will open at 50% capacity.
- Parking lots will open with protocols to follow.

These changes were to be gradual and subject to change, depending on case numbers. On May 11, government officials would determine if more changes would be imposed.

Singapore was used by the Ministry of Health as a cautionary example. It went from being a global success story to having the largest number of cases in Southeast Asia, a spike that occurred possibly because it lacked established protocols for immigrant workers. Immigrant workers were said to be one of the most highly infected groups. The nature of their work and living conditions (often in overcrowded apartments) made it challenging, if not impossible, to socially distance. Thus, Singapore had to reinstate their lockdown protocols.

10th C.R. INTERVENTION: ACTIVATE TESTING AND CONTACT TRACING

By April 30, Costa Rica had recorded 719 cases, 6 deaths, 338 recovered, and 8688 rejected cases, with a total of 13,240 completed tests. We showed a downward trajectory for several weeks and, for several days, we had more patients recovered than infected.

In what may have seemed like an effort to rationalize their own high case numbers, the President of El Salvador criticized Costa Rica for not testing enough, asserting that, if its testing rate was at El Salvador's levels, Costa Rica would have just as many or maybe more cases. By early May, when this report came out, El Salvador had completed around 30,000 tests, Panama 35,000 and Costa Rica 14,000. The Costa Rican Minister of Health addressed this critique, explaining the strategy they used for testing.

According to Daniel Salas, during the beginning of the outbreak, Costa Rica tested aggressively, up to 2500 tests per day, because they had fewer variables to look for. In the beginning they did not know much about the symptoms of the virus, where the hot spots would be, and demographics, amongst other variables. As the outbreak progressed, Costa Rica was working with more variables that allowed them to use their tests more efficiently. For example, they prioritized testing public transportation workers, as well as targeting call centers, places frequented by the elderly, and airports. They also conducted contact tracing with those individuals who were already infected with the virus to identify ripples of possible spread. They monitored and tested in healthcare centers called E.B.A.I.S (Basic Teams for Medical Attention) where influenza and other bacteria and viruses such as diarrhea had spiked in past years or were currently spiking. They were also starting to test wastewaters for the virus in different counties to help determine where to focus anti-virus efforts.

Monitoring spikes or lack of spikes of viruses and bacteria would provide a good indicator of whether or not the country's population was social distancing. In other words, Costa Rica's approach to reducing the spread of the virus was not solely dependent on testing but also testing and analyzing other related spikes and indicators to focus on enforcing protocols in those districts.

Below is the E.B.A.I.S in my town, where I will go for my social security flu shot.

Image 15. National Free Healthcare Center

IN OTHER COSTA RICAN NEWS

April 6 marked the one-month anniversary since the first case of the virus was identified in Costa Rica. At that point, we had 454 cases and two deaths. My sister and I alternated buying food and supplies for my mom and stepdad. It was my turn this day. I woke up very early to be one of the first ones at the grocery store. It wasn't too busy inside, not too many people. The store had run out of a few things, like flour and cream cheese, but it was no big deal. At my mom's, we were careful to distance ourselves. Even so, I was excited to see them, even under these circumstances. Thankfully, they were both in good health. That day I felt very grateful that Costa Rica still had food in the stores and that I could see my mom and her husband in good health.

Also on this day, according to Healthpolicy-watch news, the World Health Organization (WHO) thanked our

President, Carlos Alvarado, and the health minister, Daniel Salas, for their proposal to create a set of rights for tests, medicines and vaccines, with free access or licenses on reasonable and affordable terms for all countries. The World Health Organization supported the proposal and reported they were looking forward to having Costa Rica complete the details. The director of WHO: "Poorer countries and fragile economies stand to face the biggest shock from this pandemic, and leaving anyone unprotected will only prolong the health crisis and harm economies more."

On April 7, the news reported that 600,000 protective plastic masks were being produced here in Costa Rica, co-funded by Costa Rica social security and the private sector. The plan was to distribute 1000 masks per week. I was proud to see that report. That same day was World Health Day, celebrating doctors and nurses and healthcare staff across the world. One news report showed healthcare workers around Costa Rica clapping for several minutes, not only at hospitals but at nursing homes and clinics as well. There was news footage of the same thing happening all around the world. I remember feeling incredibly grateful for these frontline workers and clapping by myself as I watched them on TV.

On a side note, China also lifted the 76-day lockdown on Wuhan on this day, although some restrictions were still in place. This was also good news, as it provided me with some hope of normality. The Chinese government also warned, though, that the threat of further infections remained far from over.

04.08.2020
LOCAL STREET ARTIST DIES

On April 8, it devastated me to hear that Francisco Munguia, one of my favorite local street artists, had died at the age of 43. It is easy to spot Munguia's work as you walk or drive around Costa Rica. He had painted over 100 murals all over the country. He lived with the philosophy that "art can be a transformational tool for society." His murals are fun, bright, curvy, and often with animal characters.

He would often paint murals to collect funds for the rights of children and animals. When his death was reported, it was a sad day for me. I have to remind myself that his art lives on. I will remember Francisco Munguia and his gift of art to the country every time I see one of those fantastic, whimsical murals.

04.15.2020
PURIFIED ANTIBODIES

On April 15, I was thrilled to hear news about a possible treatment. The Institute Clodomiro Picado of the University of Costa Rica was spearheading the treatment of the virus in Latin America, using plasma of recovered patients as well as plasma, surprisingly, from horses. According to the Institute, it works like this: 1. The horse is immunized with non-infectious SARS-CoV2 virus proteins. 2. The plasma is then separated. 3. The anti-SARS-CoV2 antibodies are purified. 4. Vials are obtained and the drug is supplied to the severely sick.

Image 17. COVID-19 Plasma Serum Process

This Institute has over 50 years of experience producing anti-venom serum. Costa Rica has several poisonous species of animals, including frogs and snakes and accidents happen all the time. So, the Institute was already tooled up, and it was fairly easy for them to repurpose their efforts to help combat the virus. Encouraging news!

04.23.2020
PRODUCING NATIONAL PRODUCTS

On April 23, news came out that Costa Rica would start producing its own virus test kits, available within six weeks, according to the Minister of Health. There was high demand for test kits all around the world, most especially, it seemed, from China. But this activity was happening everywhere, with nations beginning to produce test kits, tracing tools, and other critical virus related products. I hoped it might become a turning point globally, not just for now, but in a post-pandemic world as well, such that countries could begin to lessen their dependence on Chinese products.

04.26.2020
COSTA RICA RECEIVES AID FROM CHINA

According to La Nación newspaper, on April 26, the first plane (since the virus hit) coming from China landed in Costa Rica – it was carrying 40 tons of badly needed supplies. These included disposable medical gowns, disposable N95 respirators, disposable masks, disposable needles, disposable gloves, and security boots for doctors and nurses. The total donation of 55 tons of supplies were to come in two other planes; total value $830.000.

IN OTHER GLOBAL NEWS

By April 3, Ecuador had become the epicenter of Latin America. Ecuador is one of the poorest countries in Latin America, with weak infrastructure and spotty healthcare. On February 29, an Ecuadorian woman returning home from Spain was identified as the first case in the country. By March 14, borders had been closed to all foreigners. There were 28 cases and two deaths at the time. Although the border closing occurred quickly, there wasn't similar timely action to shut down businesses and to limit crowds. It wasn't until March 24, almost a month after their first case, that Ecuador dismantled open markets to limit larger groups coming together. Testing was also a problem; there simply weren't enough kits for such a rapid outbreak.

By April 9, the State of New York had more cases than Italy, Spain, or any other country in the world. It was truly incredible to see these numbers go up so quickly in New York. It was hard to even relate to the numbers as representing humans; it felt out of control. The United States had over 436,000 cases, accounting for a third of the world's total infections. The US death toll was at 15,600, second only to Italy's 18,000. Two days later, the US death toll would surpass Italy.

On April 9, Costa Rica marked our highest number of cases in a day with 37. According to the Ministry of Health, this may have been the result of actions people took weeks earlier, when many escaped to the beaches for holidays. Although not entirely unexpected, the number, like much of the virus-related news, still caught us off guard.

04.22.2020
EARTH DAY

Earth Day never seemed more appreciated – celebrations were occurring all over the planet, and Earth mini-renewals of every sort seemed possible. It was refreshing to see so much Earth Day talk on the news, on the internet…it all seemed more significant. It felt like it was the only thing good that had come out of the pandemic so far. Goodnewsnetwork.org reported that the world is a greener place than it was 20 years ago and data from NASA satellites revealed this to be true. The satellite data shows that the two countries of China and India, both with the world's biggest populations, are leading the improvement in restoring the land.

Earth Day 2020 also featured Pope Francis speaking about the importance of our Earth: "We must, then, rethink how we approach the earth. Rather than exploit it for resources," … "we must remember that we stand on holy ground." The pope said that "we are capable of global responses. We have seen collective action in our response to the pandemic by showing solidarity with one another and embracing the most vulnerable in our midst" (earthday.org).

Image 19. Pope Francis

04.30.2020
THE VACCINE RACE, EXPLAINED

Producing an effective vaccine can be challenging, time-consuming, and controversial. The pandemic seemed to heighten all of this. Bill Gates has been involved in trying to help people understand the issues. In his blog GatesNotes, he discusses the processes and length of time required to produce a vaccine ("The Vaccine Race, Explained"). He wrote, "Although eighteen months might sound like a long time, this would be the fastest scientists have created a new vaccine. Development usually takes around five years. Once you pick a disease to target, you have to create the vaccine and test it on animals. Then you begin testing for safety and efficacy in humans." In other words, how well the vaccine protects you from getting sick.

We all want safe vaccines and of course we want them to be effective. But even with current vaccines that are safely administered to millions of people, efficacy isn't 100%. According to Gates, the flu vaccine is only around 45 percent effective. So, it is crucial to follow a proven process, essential for ensuring the highest safety and efficacy outcomes possible. According to the GatesNotes the process goes as follows

1. **Phase one** is the safety trial in which a small group of healthy volunteers gets the vaccine. They administer different dosages to find the one that works best.

2. **Phase two** tells you how well the vaccine worked with a small group of volunteers. If effective, hundreds of people get the vaccine (people of different ages and health statuses).

3. **Phase three** is given to thousands of people, waiting to see if it reduces how many people get sick. This phase takes more time than the other phases.

Once the vaccine is proven to work, it is submitted to the WHO and other governmental agencies for approval and mass production of the vaccine begins. Gates said, "So, to speed up the process, vaccine developers are compressing the timeline."

The article mentions that as of April 9, 115 different vaccine candidates are in the development pipeline. He thinks 8 or 10 of those look promising. It delighted me to read this article as it provided a bit of hope. I had a newfound appreciation for all the scientists in the world who are working on this effort.

CHAPTER IX

New York's Reaction

I believe it's important to cover how the US state of New York reacted to the pandemic, because it says to leaders everywhere that, no matter how upside-down things are, it's never too late to get in front of needed change. The State's Governor Andrew Cuomo exemplifies a leader who took responsibility through adversity.

The irony of this is that New York had China, Italy, Spain and other countries as bellringers of what could happen to them, weeks before being hit with the virus. It could have been deduced that urgency was required. But, Governor Cuomo did not create urgency, at least initially. According to the *New York Times*, he said "Excuse our arrogance as New Yorkers — I speak for the mayor on this one — we think we have the best health care system on the planet right here in New York. So, when you're saying what happened in other countries versus what happened here, we don't even think it's going to be as bad as it was in other countries."

Image 20. Andrew Cuomo

We now know that New York was not ready. In fact, it appeared dangerously ill-prepared. Even with several cases already confirmed, shut downs were not put in place. Testing was iffy, and there was no mandate for social distancing protocols.

In my opinion, no US leader, not even the medical experts, created the urgency needed to effect change. Governor Cuomo could have made critical decisions earlier, thus preventing unnecessary spread of the virus. For example, it wasn't until the end of March that New York City closed most subways and public transportation, a latency of more than 20 days after the first case popped up in New York City. That mistake alone let the virus spread quickly throughout New York, infecting, and, in many cases, leading to the death of, hundreds of people.

There was similar footage coming out of China, Italy, and Spain; the virus was spreading like wildfire. Once again, the news would show hospitals at full capacity. Doctors and nurses were pleading for supplies. Digging of mass graves in

Hart Island, New York increased rapidly and corpses had to be stored in container trucks, some without refrigeration. On March 14, New York reported its first virus death. By April 30ꞏ the number was 23,780. It was incredibly sad to watch.

Image 21 Refrigerated containers for the dead in NYC

GOVERNOR CUOMO'S ROAD TO REDEMPTION USING STOP, PREPARE, ACT

Every morning, I would watch Governor Cuomo walk into a sizeable room filled with reporters. He had a calm and confident manner about him. A little too calm for my taste, especially in the beginning. Nevertheless, he showed great courage and leadership in confronting the warlike situation they were in. He never blamed others, nor did he blame himself, but most importantly he *Stopped* everything that was status quo. This signaled that change was needed. He communicated their current situation using daily slide shows. He explained what would happen if they kept going in the current direction and what would happen if they were able to flatten the curve. He *Prepared*; he communicated a strategy. He explained what needed to happen next and plans for carrying it out. He answered questions from the media. He delivered a consistent message and eventually led the change versus react to it and was able to *Act* to implement his plan.

Because of his leadership, by mid-June, New York had become one of the safest states and cities in the US in terms of the impact. While most of the country was spiking dramatically, New York had flattened the curve. This is an outstanding example that it's never too late to manage change, even if it looks impossible.

CHAPTER X

April – #Liberate

When we talk about change, we're really talking about two issues. One is the event that's happening that requires a response; in other words, the change to be dealt with. The second, of course, is the change-related behavior(s) that we engage in order to mitigate, advance, or in some way deal with the change. In contrast to the actions taken by New York's Governor Cuomo, President Trump decided to not lead the fundamental change, the pandemic, that was coming our way. Stopping the spread should have been paramount, but this wasn't a strategic priority. Citing uneven levels of cases across the various states, Trump refused to issue a stay-at-home order that would apply to all, and that decision alone had severe ramifications.

Instead, Trump promoted a different change, that of reopening the economy as soon as possible. By April 1, he was pushing this very hard. From a change management standpoint, he did a great job creating urgency and communicating and familiarizing US citizens about what was coming. But, it was disastrous that his timing and prioritization was so off. In fact, the thing that *should* have been a Federally-managed top priority...equipment to halt the virus's spread...didn't seem to be on his radar screen at all. By early April, the availability of ventilators, protective masks, and testing kits had become a massive problem in New York and in many other states around the country. Instead of leaving profitability and politics aside for the sake of getting in front of the pandemic, President Trump made a reckless decision-of-omission that effectively resulted in a bidding war between states for badly needed equipment. He could have used the Defense Production Act to compel industries to help with the construction of ventilators, masks and other supplies that were sorely needed across the country. But he didn't. In order to obtain these essential pieces of equipment, states found themselves bidding against each other, as a handful of distributors controlled the scarce supply.

Demand was high. New York alone had around 76,000 thousand cases and 1,550 deaths. The notion of "We the people" seemed to have disappeared, as governors, mayors, and other leaders scrambled to provide for their own citizens. We were witnessing capitalism at its worst, an unwitting outcome to an ill-advised disregard for top-down management of a national disaster. Governor Cuomo said, "You now literally will have a company call you up and say, 'Well, California just outbid you.' "It's like being on eBay, with 50 other states bidding on a ventilator." New York City alone was asking for 30,000 ventilators. These types of demands drove the prices of such vital equipment sky high. As a result, well-resourced states were able to buy what they needed, while poorer states received very little. Capitalizing and profiteering during a national emergency was a new low for the US and for the world. And people paid the price. Some with their lives, which is unconscionable. And the rest of us… with having to un-remember examples of greed,

imprudence, and lack of compassion by those in power in times of distress.

04.01.2020
MICHIGAN REACHES 3RD PLACE

The first Michigan case popped up on March 10, with the first death nine days later on March 19. I remember being surprised by the short time between the first case and the first death. On that same day, the number of cases jumped to 324, up from the previous day's 80 reported cases. Twelve days after that, there were 7,615 cases and 259 deaths, and this is how Michigan became third in the country by April 1.

I worried about my parents as they are both in their 70's. Luckily, neither of them has respiratory problems, and they don't live near what was then the epicenter, Detroit. I do, however, have an aunt, uncle, and cousins in that area. When, I called them to see how they were doing, they said people were getting sick and dying left and right. I told them to please stay safe; there wasn't much else I could do.

I asked myself why the virus had exploded in Michigan, not in Chicago, where there is more population, more foot traffic, and travelers. I did a little research. According to Dr. Joneigh Khaldun, Michigan's Chief Medical Executive: "One factor was the increase in testing compared to other places. When Michigan confirmed its first cases on March 10th, the state had only 300 test kits, and the State Bureau of Laboratories was processing all the tests. Soon they would test hundreds more. But the rapidly rising numbers aren't just a reflection of more testing."

Dr. Teena Chopra, an infectious disease specialist for the Detroit Medical Center, said on CNN, "...the high poverty rate in Detroit and some of the surrounding communities means that people are less likely to seek medical attention unless they are very sick." Dr. Paul Kilgore, a medical doctor and epidemiologist at Detroit-area Wayne State University, said, "That high poverty rate also means people may not have heard about the state's stay-at-home order or the social distancing guidelines or may be less in a position to adhere to them."

04.02.2020
THE RACIAL BREAKDOWN

On April 2, Michigan's Department of Health and Human Services started releasing official data showing the racial breakdown of cases and deaths. It would be eye-opening to the world that the virus was not equally affecting everyone. The data showed that, although just 14% of the population of Michigan is black, 33% of cases and 41% of deaths were in the black community.

More data would come out in the weeks ahead from other parts of the country. It became evident that the pandemic was not impacting everyone equally. It was hitting minorities in poor communities where healthcare was lacking or where it was difficult to access accurate information. This access-gap is a socioeconomic and healthcare problem not only in the US, but around the world.

On April 10, President Trump said during the White House Task Force briefing, that he didn't feel the need for extensive testing in order to reopen the US economy. In response, Gov. Cuomo stated he would not open New York's economy unless "we start testing at a mass scale or else we will have a relapse and another spike." This argument concerning how and when to open the economy would cause a national division of opinion, policy, and compliance across the United States in the days to come.

04.16.2020
#LIBERATE MICHIGAN

Again, I woke to a tweet forwarded to me from a friend. It said, "Michigan Proud Boys, organized a blockade of the

68

intersection at a green light outside of Sparrow Hospital. A doctor came out to plead with them to let the ambulances through." There was a picture of the doctor in the middle of the car blockade. I could not believe what I was reading. I looked into a bit more, and indeed it was true. Less than a month after Governor Whitmer had placed a statewide lockdown, thousands of people were protesting in the capital, Lansing, a place I know well. As a kid, I would ride my bike around the Michigan State University campus. I also have friends and family in that area. It greatly embarrassed me to see what was happening there.

Image 22. Dr. Asking protestors to let ambulance through

Footage that was hard to watch: Protesters not social distancing, demanding that Democratic Governor Gretchen Whitmer end her strict stay-at-home orders because it restricts their freedom. I watched angry demonstrators waving Confederate flags out of their car windows and chanting 'lock her up'. Unbelievably, some were holding machine guns. A traffic blockade stretched for miles. I recall seeing a man complaining about not being able to buy birdseed and woman complaining about not being able to go to the hair salon, apparently a "necessity" because her gray roots were showing.

According to dailymail.co.uk, Michigan's Governor criticized the protesters for risking themselves and others by taking part in the protest by touching each other, handing out food with their bare hands, and blocking an ambulance. She also said, "it was ironic that a group rallying against her stay-at-home order may have just created a reason to lengthen it."

04.17.2020
TRUMP RETWEETS

The following morning on April 17, President Trump retweeted "#LiberateMinnesota," followed by another tweet, "#LiberateMichigan," and then "#Liberate Virginia." He was egging on the protestors in these swing states and undercutting his administration's guidelines of social-distancing. He was once again putting his political agenda ahead of the health of the American people. It had an effect. In the following days, we would see hundreds of protesters in several states across the US.

I realized their frustration and the need to have an income; I was living in the same situation. I also understand that economies need to rebuild. Nevertheless, there is a safe way to do things and it requires short-term sacrifice on the part of all of us. It's hard to understand why this is so difficult for some people. Maybe it's the "short-term" part. Maybe it's the "sacrifice" that's just anathema on its face. But the outcomes are clear. Refusing to socially distance puts their safety and the safety of others at stake. And there's a lot to be lost in opening up an economy prematurely, and in a disorderly fashion.

04/18/2020
TOGETHER AT HOME CONCERT

On April 17, the Republic of Ireland quadrupled its contribution to the World Health Organization (WHO), a response to the Trump administration pulling out of WHO. The next day, the protest gained prominent international support when Lady Gaga organized the 'Together At Home' concert for the pandemic relief. World-renowned performers including Paul McCartney, Rolling Stones, Stevie Wonder, and John Legend came together to entertain the world and to help raise over 128 million dollars, a strong show of support in this time of critical worldwide need.

04/30/2020
THE SOCIALLY IRRESPONSIBLE ARE BACK

By April 30, protests and anger had increased all across the US, some for and some against rules and restrictions that were being imposed to prevent the spread of the virus. As soon as safety protocols were put in place, they were broken by some and defended by others. One example was California, where Governor Gavin Newsom had loosened restrictions on beaches and parks, but with social distancing requirements. When people immediately broke protocols and filled the beaches, Newsom closed them down again.

Michigan was also back in the news, showing thousands of protestors storming the Capitol in Lansing. Some brandished Confederate flags, swastikas, nooses, and firearms. Governor Gretchen Whitmer responded on CNN: "Some of the outrageousness of what happened at our Capitol depicted some of the worst racism and awful parts of our history in this country..." They were protesting because they did not want restrictions extended, from April 30 to May 28.

In the middle of this, President Trump tweeted, "The Governor of Michigan should give a little, and put out the fire. These are very good people, but they are angry. They want their lives back again, safely! See them, talk to them, make a deal." To me, Trump's comments were in the same vein as those he made about the racially-charged protesters in Charlottesville, Virginia. People may recall this, when a car plowed into a crowd protesting white nationalism. Referring to those supporting a nationalism agenda, President Trump said then, "But not all of those people were neo-Nazis, believe me. Not all of those people were white supremacists, by any stretch. Those people were also there because they wanted to protest the taking down of a statue of Robert E. Lee."

Hours before the state of emergency was to expire on April 30, Michigan's Governor Whitmer signed a series of executive orders in an attempt to curtail the spread of the virus. She said, "...in some counties in western and northern Michigan, cases are doubling every six days or faster." "By refusing to extend the emergency and disaster declaration, Republican lawmakers are putting their heads in the sand and putting more lives and livelihoods at risk. I'm not going to let that happen." To me, Governor Gretchen Whitmer is a genuine leader who did not back down even when her life was in danger. Her actions were critically important, because, by May 1, the State of Michigan had 41,000 cases and almost 4000 deaths.

Personal note: As I mentioned before, I lived in Michigan for a while in my youth. I went to high school there and I have friends and family still there. Like most places in the US, Michigan is made up of people who represent lots of different nationalities and many types of beliefs. I can say from experience that gun-slinging, swastika-wearing protesters are not the norm in Michigan. The State has 10 million people, and these protesters number just a couple of thousand. They're noticeable because they represent the extreme. But there are millions of others who aim for the reasonable middle. To give you a personal example, my sweet stepmother, from a small town in Michigan, had been hand-making protective masks and donating them to hospitals, friends, and family for weeks. She said she would keep on doing so until they tell her that they no longer need them. She even sent some to my family and me here in Costa Rica.

CHAPTER XI

April – Dr. Anthony Fauci

Image 23 Dr. Fauci

Dr. Anthony Fauci is arguably the preeminent immunologist in the United States. As such, he was appointed by President Trump to the White House Task Force. From the start, there were discrepant messages to the public coming from the White House and the President versus his Task Force. Admittedly, it was a careful dance that Task Force experts were engaged in, trying to put forth science-based information while not openly contradicting statements coming from the Trump Administration. Around mid-April, Dr. Fauci began to make statements that were more pointed, more directive, and more cautionary than those in prior months. It was a hopeful sign. From a change management point of view, I believe he would have liked to *Stop, Prepare, and Act* for a second wave. Unfortunately, his recommendations were overshadowed by President Trump's push to reopen the economy, inexplicably set for Easter Sunday (April 12). On this day, the US had reported over half a million cases, 527,175 to be exact, and there had been 20,473 deaths. Both numbers led the world, surpassing even pandemic-wracked Italy. In a carefully worded statement that signaled a rebuttal to the Administration's arbitrary Easter timeline, Dr. Fauci said, "…there is a good possibility that there should be parts of the US that will go back to normal by May. It's not a one size fits all."

04.12.2020
FAUCI INTERVIEW WITH CNN

On April 12, Dr. Fauci sat for an interview with well-known television journalist Jake Tapper. Trying to get at the reason for such widely-discrepant case numbers in various parts of the world, Tapper asked, "South Korea and the US both confirmed their first case around the same time. If you look now, the US has 50 thousand more cases and almost 100 thousand more deaths… is it because we started too late in the US?" Fauci replied, "It's not as simple as that, but where we are right now is because of a number of factors, the size of the country… It's a bit unfair to compare the US to South Korea, where they had an outbreak in Daegu, and they had the capability to immediately shut it off completely, in a way that we may not have been able to do in this country. So obviously, it would have been nice if we had a better head start, but I don't think you can say that we are where we are now because of one factor."

Tapper: "Experts such as yourself and other top officials wanted to recommend social and physical distancing guidelines to President Trump as far back as the third week of February, but the administration didn't announce these guidelines until March 16th almost a month later. Why?" Fauci said, "we look at it from a pure health standpoint, make a recommendation, often the recommendation is taken, sometimes it's not. It is what it is. We are where we are right now."

The journalist then asked him directly, "Do you think lives could have been saved if social distancing, physical distancing, stay-at-home measures would have started the third week of February rather than mid-March?" Fauci: "You know Jake it's the 'what would have,' the 'what could have,' it's very difficult to go back and say that, I mean you could logically say that if you had a process that was ongoing and you started mitigation earlier, you could have saved lives. Obviously, no one is going to deny that. But what goes into those kinds of decisions is complicated, but you are right. If we had right from the very beginning, shut everything down, it may have been a little bit different, but there were a lot of pushbacks about shutting things down." Hours later, President Trump retweeted "Time to #FireFauci."

The next day during the White House news briefing, Dr. Fauci tried to clarify what he had meant in the Tapper interview. He was obviously in an uncomfortable position, not being able to provide accurate information to the US citizens, and shouldering the not-unreasonable risk of being fired. The same news briefing saw growing pressure from the media to have President Trump explain the lost month of February, a time of Federally-based inaction in terms of preparing for the outbreak. In the middle of the briefing, something unprecedented happened. President Trump asked for the lights to be dimmed. For the next few minutes, reporters, US citizens, and people all over the world were shown a Fox News promotional video of the President. It seemed inappropriately political at such a time when the country, all its citizens regardless of their politics, needed a comprehensive, all-inclusive response to the pandemic threat – an effective plan that applied to all. It also felt to me as an act of desperation.

04.19.2020
EXPERTS' GUIDELINES TO REOPEN

I was pleased to see some Change Management actions coming from the White House. Early on, there had been only a desperate, "reactive" reaction to the pandemic. With the establishment of the White House Task Force, guidelines for a proactive response were put forth, and, via this document, Dr. Fauci and the other scientists provided a plan to prepare for the reopening of the US economy.

The first and most crucial step in the four-step plan is to meet all Gaiting Criteria, a requirement before moving into Phases 1, 2, and 3 of the Task Force Guidelines.

Gaiting Criteria Symptoms:
- The downward trajectory of influenza-like illness (ILI) reported within 14 days.
- The downward trajectory of virus-like symptoms cases reported within 14 days.

Gaiting Criteria Cases:
- The downward trajectory of documented cases within 14 days or a downward trajectory of positive tests as a percent of the total tests within the 14 days.

Gaiting Criteria Hospitals:
- Treat all patients without crisis care.
- Robust testing program in place for at-risk healthcare workers, including emerging antibody testing.

The Criteria were essential for helping states know when and how to manage their reopening plans. For example, the State of Georgia had planned to open its economy as early as

April 24. However, at about this time, they were reporting over 18,000 confirmed cases and close to 700 deaths. There was not a "downward trajectory" (per Guideline Criteria) of virus symptoms nor was there a downward trajectory of cases and deaths. The numbers were all going up. Moreover, the State was planning to open gyms, barbershops, hair salons, nail salons, massage shops, and tattoo parlors, a plan that was in conflict with Phase 1 criteria, since all these businesses require direct physical contact between the employee and the customer.

In addition to the Task Force Guidelines, there were other sources of guidance for states. Experts cited key models showing that, not only Georgia, but 11 other states should wait until at least June 8 to reopen. Adding to that warning, an April 20 Harvard Study explained that current testing levels were not at all sufficient; in fact, testing needed to *triple* before the country could safely open.

04/20/2020
DR. FAUCI WARNS THE USA

On ABC's *Good Morning America*, Dr. Fauci made a clear warning: "Unless we get the virus under control, the real recovery economically is not going to happen." "So, if you jump the gun and go into a situation where you have a big spike you're going to set yourself back."

Fauci said that, although it is painful to follow guidelines of a gradually phased reopening, moving too quickly and avoiding restrictions is going to backfire. That's the problem. As if not understanding the gravity of the situation and the need for a smart, graduated, rolled-out response to the pandemic, President Trump praised those who were flaunting the Guidelines and not complying, saying that some Governors "have gone too far" in imposing restrictions.

04.23.2020

LYSOL LIES

As Dr. Fauci was warning people about opening too soon, President Trump was discussing alternatives for treating the virus. In an April 23 press conference, President Trump appeared to be speaking to Dr. Deborah Birx, a Task Force expert, who was sitting close to him: "So, supposing when we hit the body with a tremendous, whether it's ultraviolet or just very powerful light, and I think you said that hadn't been checked, but you're going to test it. And then I said that supposing you brought the light inside the body, which you can do either through the skin or another way. And I think you said you're going to test that too. Sounds interesting. And then I see the disinfectant, where it knocks it out in a minute, one minute. And is there a way we can do something like that; by injecting it inside or almost a cleaning? Because you see, it gets in the lungs and it does a tremendous number on the lungs, it'd be interesting to check that. So, you're going to have to use medical doctors with it, but it sounds interesting to me. So, we'll see, but the whole concept of the light, the way it kills it in one minute. That's pretty powerful."

In an unbelievably immediate and chaotic aftermath, hundreds of US citizens called their governors and other state officials asking if it was safe to drink or inject disinfectant as a cure for the virus. Industry reaction to the confusion and chaos was necessarily swift. Leaving little doubt that the President's remarks were preposterous and irrational, Reckitt Benckiser, the parent company of the disinfectants Lysol and Dettol, issued a statement: "As a global leader in health and hygiene products, we must be clear that under no circumstance should our disinfectant products be administered into the human body (through injection, ingestion, or any other route)," "As with all products, our disinfectant and hygiene products should only be used as intended and in line with usage guidelines. Please read the label and safety information."

04.29.2020
REMDESIVIR

A few days later, Dr. Fauci reported that early studies had showed that a drug called Remdesivir could block the effects of the virus. Remdesivir was originally developed to treat Ebola and Marburg virus. The drug blocks an enzyme that the virus needs to survive, thereby shortening the recovery time for patients. According to Fauci, the mortality rate trended better with Remdisivir, as well. He emphasized that it is a possible treatment, not a vaccine. Either way, it was significant news because the mortality rate for the virus was chilling. More US citizens had died in three months of the virus than the 16 years of the Vietnam War. More than 58,000 Americans had died at this point.

04.30.2020
DR FAUCI WARNS THE US AGAIN

On April 30, CNN interviewed Dr. Fauci regarding the 31 states that were in the process of reopening. "The concern that I have is that some states are leapfrogging over the first checkpoint." He was referring to the Gaiting Criteria from the Task Force's Guidelines, the first checkpoint that required 14 days of decreased cases, deaths, and symptoms in order to consider next steps in Change Management (such as reopening). I hoped the US would not make the same mistake twice of putting economy over science during an uncontained pandemic, but unfortunately, they did just that.

By April 30, thirty-one states were partially reopening. None of these states had met either the Gaiting Criteria or Phase 1 of the experts' guidelines. On this day, Johns Hopkins University reported that the US had reached over 1 million cases, from a total of 3 million globally. With less than 5% of the world's population, the United States accounted for one-third of the infections.

CHAPTER XII

April – Economy, Science and Deaths

Horrifying news from Guayaquil, Ecuador (population approximately 3 million) spread across Latin America during the month of April. Hospitals became overcrowded to the point that ambulances, firefighters, and police stopped picking up the sick or the dead. There was footage of doctors and nurses, who were also getting infected and dying, writing goodbye letters to their families. By the second week of April, there were 6700 deaths in Guayaquil; over 300 corpses had been left in their houses for days. Media footage showed corpses on the streets. Families would have to wrap the bodies of their loved ones in whatever material they had and leave them on the streets. Eventually, private companies started distributing cardboard coffins. Mass graves were dug in public parks. It was heartbreaking to see.

Unforgettable images; people were just keeling over. I especially remember a news segment showing an older, heavy-set man, selling lotto tickets on a bench, suddenly just

Image 25. Dead person left on street in Ecuador

slumping to the ground. The Ecuadorian journalist broke down crying in the middle of the broadcast, pleading with people to stay home. I, too, broke down in tears that night. The next day similar footage of mass graves came out of Brazil, another country that had denied the severity of the pandemic. I could only think of the ticking time bomb to our north, Nicaragua.

SCIENCE V. ECONOMY

This was the dilemma countries were facing once the pandemic started, and it was ongoing. Some countries downplayed scientific facts and data and became severely devastated to the point that they shut down their entire economy. Some countries respected the science, using data as a guide to strictly prepare for the change that was coming. As a result, those countries, Costa Rica among them, were able to avoid complete economic shutdowns, keeping some sectors of business and industry operating.

However, by mid-April, it appeared the world was once again in the calm before the storm, as a probable second wave approached. Just as before, we were facing the same crossroad of action, economy then science or science then economy. Last time, it didn't work very well for those that prioritized economy over science. Countries that adhered to science-based data and directives were doing better off economically and as far as death count than those that had not.

Germany, for example, had taken a scientific approach since the beginning, not a surprise since Chancellor Angela Merkel is a trained physicist. Her stance was that Germany should do everything possible to slow the spread, thereby winning time to develop a vaccine and for people to develop immunity and to allow the healthcare system to build capacity, thus keeping it from becoming overwhelmed. Merkel also sought advice from her experts, such as Dr. Lothar Wielder. According to the *New York Times* in March, Wielder explained the advantages of allowing capacity to build: "But every one of us can figure out that the longer this takes, the better it is. On the one hand, because then the chance that a vaccine will become available increases, and on the other hand, because there is a chance that treatments will be available."

Sweden, on the other hand, had prioritized its economy, depending on the healthcare system to handle their cases. They approached the pandemic with a philosophy of "herd immunity" from the beginning, leaving it up to their citizens to determine their own actions and the ensuing risk of becoming infected. Restaurants, bars, barbershops - all were open. In a different approach, Portugal, whose population is similar to Sweden's, took steps to declare a state of emergency as soon as it reported the first death. Sweden never did declare a state of emergency.

Both Sweden and Portugal had around the same a time to prepare and react to the pandemic; in fact, Portugal had less time as it is closer to Italy and Spain. By April 30.

Portugal
Population 10 million
25 thousand cases

989 deaths

Sweden
Population 10 million
21 thousand cases
2,586 Deaths

The Mercury Times asked Sweden's state epidemiologist, Anders Tegnell, whether the death toll would have been lower if Sweden had followed the same path as other European countries in introducing strict restrictions. Tegnell replied: "That's a very difficult question to answer at this stage. At least 50% of our death toll is within the elderly homes, and we have a hard time understanding how a lockdown would stop the introduction of the disease into the elderly homes." This was a surprise to me because it was a very uncertain way to react to a pandemic.

THE ELDERLY

Más de la mitad de adultos mayores que contrajeron COVID-19 en el país lo vencieron y ya están recuperados

Image 26. More than half of our elderly with COVID-19 in our country, beat it and are recovered.

I believe that we should protect the elderly and respect them for their knowledge and for their lifelong efforts for future generations. The loss of so many elders during this pandemic has been tragic. No country's older population has escaped being touched by the virus. We've seen high death tolls among this demographic all over the world. But, Costa

Rica was a different story – one exemplar of positive outcomes through their science-based efforts to contain and control the pandemic. On May 3, the newspaper *El Observador* reported that more than half of Costa Rica's infected elderly (age 65+) had survived. All had been tested twice, with a wait time of 24 hours between each test before being discharged. The oldest survivor was 86 years old.

CHAPTER XIII

Test Your Traffic Light

By April 30, there were many unsettling changes in the forefront of the pandemic. Here are a few from Costa Rica and the United States.

Costa Rica:

- Our neighbor, Nicaragua, had ever-increasing numbers. Were we ready for an influx from the North, many with the virus?
- Our economy had frozen. How would we reopen safely?
- We were rapidly maxing out Social Security and the universal healthcare system; how would we mitigate this reality?
- An enormous number of our small and mid-size businesses had gone bankrupt. Would the government help them, and, if so, how?
- Hospital beds and supplies were limited. Did we have plan for supplies for a second and third wave?

- Social distancing and mask usage were both still not the norm. Will the government enforce socially distance and the use of masks?
- Testing needed to increase. Would we have enough tests?
- Contact tracing technologies, how would those work?
- How would schools and universities start up again?

USA:

- The US economy appeared headed for another great recession. How could they prevent this from happening?
- The United States had more cases and deaths than Russia, Germany, France, UK, Italy, and Spain combined. How could the number of cases and deaths be reduced?
- Thirty million Americans had filed for unemployment, which is almost the entire population of Canada. How could more jobs be created? How could people be returned to work safely?
- 2020 is an election year. How would they allow people to vote safely?
- US healthcare and the socioeconomic system were still severely broken. How would these be fixed, strengthened, or revised enough to benefit everyone?
- Many states were opening without meeting the criteria put forth by experts, risking an even harder second wave. Would hospitals be ready?
- Not enough testing was occurring and the economy was opening. Would this change?

- Social distancing and mask usage were not being enforced. Would those be?
- How would schools open safely?
- Some businesses and organizations were not providing Personal Protective Equipment (PPE's). Would this change?
- Contact tracing technologies, how would they work? Volunteer or enforced?

The rest of the world was facing similar changes, which were all unsettling. Organizations, countries, states, towns, businesses, and even households needed to prepare for the challenges ahead, those they knew about and, to the extent possible, those that were not yet fully clear. Preparation for change is key. It makes little sense to sit back and wait, especially when given the "luxury" of knowing what's coming. Although leadership helps, expecting our leaders to take care of us is not broadly proactive enough to effectively deal with change. It takes all of us to do our part in promoting a proactive plan. Of course, we need to make sure our leaders expect and plan for the difference (the change). But, we are all in this together and our collective efforts to manage the change will go a long way toward reducing negative consequences impacting us all. So, what can we do? For a start, we can demand answers from our leaders and hold them accountable, as well as to plan and to prepare ourselves. To this end, let us reflect on a couple of changes that have happened to us and determine where our leaders dropped the ball and what we could have done better.

RATE YOUR TRAFFIC LIGHT

As a Change Management Consultant and Coach, I am rarely called in to an organization to help proactively plan for change. Instead, it's more common that the organization's

89

leadership is reacting to change that has already occurred or that is in the process of occurring. They are feeling the consequence of not preparing and would like to remedy it as soon as possible. So, I begin to ask questions, to analyze what happened and how it negatively impacted the organization. In other words, I try to pinpoint where they dropped the ball, and then move forward with a change management plan. After the impact analysis, I begin taking leadership and stakeholders through the Phase Analysis process. We start with the Red phase (Stop), move on to Yellow (Prepare), and end at Green (Act).

Let's go over a couple of examples.

In the first example, think about how the USA handled the pandemic in the first 4 months. Start at the Red Phase (*Stop*). Use the 8-star rating system to score the entire phase. 0-Stars is the lowest score (no change management) and 8-Stars is the highest. For each question, place a star next to it if the behavior occurred. If it did not occur, or if you answered *no,* leave it blank. Add up all the stars at the bottom to score that phase.

EXAMPLE 1: INITIAL OUTBREAK IN USA

	Questions	Stars
Red Phase **STOP**	1. Did leaders stop and create urgency regarding the change?	
	2. Did people receive explanations of the change and when it was most likely to happen?	
	3. Were leaders leading an actionable response to the change? (The Outbreak)	
	4. Were those that were identified as being medium to highly impacted warned about the change coming? *This would include groups such as First Responders, The Elderly, Essential Workers, Transportation Industry and so on.*	
	5. Were the impacted groups informed how and why they were identified as moderate to highly impacted?	
	6. Were they told about the consequences of not changing?	
	7. Were they told about the rewards for changing?	
	8. Did those impacted express or feel confidence in their leaders?	
	Total # of Stars	**/8**

	Questions	Stars
Yellow Phase **PREPARE**	1. Did leaders start pandemic update meetings and communicate where they are in the process and where they want to be?	
	2. Were those impacted informed exactly what would change for them? *This would include new policies, rules, protocols, equipment, processes and so on.*	
	3. Were performance improvement measures identified? *E.g. Hospital capacity, required equipment and resources and so on.*	
	4. Were they told the skills needed and training(s) to complete? *E.g. Covid 19 testing, healthcare protocol training, prevention training and so on*	
	5. Were there incentive programs in identified? *These are rewards and consequences to help with a smooth translon of the change.*	
	6. Were barriers that might impact the change management identified, mitigated and communicated?	
	7. Did those that were impacted feel that the organization was ready for the change?	
	8. Did those impacted feel confident in their leader(s)?	
	Total # of Stars	**/8**

	Questions	Stars
Green Phase **ACT**	1. Did leaders continue pandemic update meetings and communicate where they are in the process and where they want to be?	
	2. Did leadership launch/begin the Change Management Strategy?	
	3. Were performance improvement measures implemented? *E.g. Enough hospital capacity, required equipment and resources.*	
	4.Were those impacted performing the required skills needed to help adapt to the change?	
	5.Were there incentive programs in place and working? *These are rewards and consequences to help adapt to the change.*	
	6.Were barriers that are impacting the change management being mitigated?	
	7. Did those that were impacted feel that the organization was handling the change appropriately?	
	8. Did those impacted feel confident in their leader(s)?	
	Total # of Stars	**/8**

What phase was your first phase that received a score of 4 stars or fewer? _____

Here's how I rated each Phase.

	Questions	Stars
Red Phase **STOP**	1. Did leaders stop and create urgency regarding the change?	
	2. Did people receive explanations of the change and when it was most likely to happen?	
	3. Were leaders leading an actionable response to the change? (The Outbreak)	
	4. Were those that were identified as being medium to highly impacted warned about the change coming? *This would include groups such as First Responders, The Elderly, Essential Workers, Transportation Industry and so on.*	
	5. Were the impacted groups informed how and why they were identified as moderate to highly impacted?	
	6. Were they told about the consequences of not changing?	
	7. Were they told about the rewards for changing?	
	8. Did those impacted express or feel confidence in their leaders?	
	Total # of Stars	**0/8**

Reasons for my scoring of the **Stop** Phase 0/8 :
- Leadership did not create a sense of urgency nor did they communicate the potential impact of the outbreak. They also did not warn the highly impacted industries.
- They did not explain when and where it was most likely to spread. E.g. public transportation, mass gathering
- They did not manage the change on a daily basis.
- They did not provide constant communication about the change.

- They did not communicate the benefits of adapting to the change or the consequences.

	Questions	Stars
Yellow Phase **PREPARE**	1. Did leaders start pandemic update meetings and communicate where they are in the process and where they want to be?	
	2. Were those impacted informed exactly what would change for them? *This would include new policies, rules, protocols, equipment, processes and so on.*	
	3. Were performance improvement measures identified? *E.g. Hospital capacity, required equipment and resources and so on.*	
	4.Were they told the skills needed and training(s) to complete? *E.g. Covid 19 testing, healthcare protocol training, prevention training and so on*	
	5.Were there incentive programs in identified? *These are rewards and consequences to help with a smooth translon of the change.*	
	6.Were barriers that might impact the change management identified, mitigated and communicated?	
	7. Did those that were impacted feel that the organization was ready for the change?	
	8. Did those impacted feel confident in their leader(s)?	
	Total # of Stars	**0/8**

Reasons for my **Prepare** Phase scoring **0/8**:
- There were pandemic update meetings, but these meetings were non-actionable.
- Those impacted were not informed about changes to them. E.g., New policies, equipment, tests, processes, curfews, social distancing

- Leaders downplayed the change and people did not feel ready. Some didn't feel the need to prepare.
- There were no performance improvement measures in place to support the change. E.g., Hospital capacity, enough resources and equipment
- They never communicated which trainings were needed. E.g., Healthcare guidelines, testing training, contact tracing, best practices, processes.

		Questions	Stars
Green Phase **ACT**		1. Did leaders continue pandemic update meetings and communicate where they are in the process and where they want to be?	
		2. Did leadership launch/begin the Change Management Strategy?	
		3. Were performance improvement measures implemented? *E.g. Enough hospital capacity, required equipment and resources.*	
		4. Were those impacted performing the required skills needed to help adapt to the change?	
		5. Were there incentive programs in place and working? *These are rewards and consequences to help adapt to the change.*	
		6. Were barriers that are impacting the change management being mitigated?	
		7. Did those that were impacted feel that the organization was handling the change appropriately?	
		8. Did those impacted feel confident in their leader(s)?	
		Total # of Stars	**0/8**

Reasons for my **Act** Phase scoring 0/8:

- There were few actionable pandemic update meetings. (They did recommend hand washing but little else.)
- No change management strategy was implemented. E.g. Communication plan, training program
- Needed resources were not put in place.
- Necessary supplies were not ordered or received in a timely manner.
- There were no readiness surveys.
- They did not have an incentive program (consequences, rewards).

The **Red Phase (Stop)** was the first phase with a score of 4 stars or below.

In Example 1, all stages earned poor scores from me. Change was managed poorly, and as we all know, many Americans did not take a proactive stance nor did they adapt well to the change. People were caught by surprise and, regrettably, the consequences were severe.

To deal with these problems, we look at phases that received 4-stars or fewer. We start with the first phase that received 4-Stars or fewer, and then go to the next phase that scored 4-Stars or fewer, and so on. In this example, the Red Phase (Stop) was the first phase. So how do we address Red Phase issues so that we do not make the same mistakes again?

Well, for starters, we can demand that leadership provide us with details on what their plan is and when will it be implemented. This means pressing for responses from *all* leaders, including state senators and representatives, state governors, city officials, CEOs, Managers, and Executive branch leaders, including the President. We need to ask questions that require answers with actionable responses, in order to be strategically prepared before we have to deal with the next pandemic, outbreak, or wave.

- Where is the next epicenter or wave most likely to happen, and why?
- When and how will you create awareness and urgency for the next outbreak, wave, or epicenter?
- Which individuals, groups, industries, departments are likely to be most impacted?
- What protocols will be communicated when this happens?
- When will these protocols be implemented?
- What are possible consequences for our citizens for not following protocols (besides catching the virus)?
- What are the benefits for adequately preparing?

At the workplace, for example, employees could consider asking these urgent questions of their managers, supervisors, and CEOs.

- What percentage of employees will have the ability to work remotely?
- When should we exclude workers or visitors from the workspace?
- Should we revise our benefits policies in cases employees are barred from the worksite or we close it?
- Do we have reliable systems for real-time public health communication with employees?
- When should we revise our policies around international and domestic business travel?
- When should we postpone or cancel scheduled live conferences or meetings?

- When will supervisors be adequately trained for the next wave or pandemic?

Please note that it's critical to address the <u>first</u> phase that has been rated below 4-Stars before tackling other low-score phases. It would be unproductive to spend resources (time, money, effort) to try to mitigate the next phase because the fundamentals wouldn't have yet been addressed. For example, if you do not *Stop!* and address Red Phase issues and, instead, skip to the Yellow *Prepare* Phase when the Red Phases issues are deficient, it's likely that people may not prepare adequately or even feel it's important to do so. Each phase builds off the next to assure that change is successful.

Let's look at another example. Again, rate each phase starting from the Red Phase using the 8-Star rating system. Total your stars at the bottom of each table.

EXAMPLE 2: USA REOPENING ECONOMY-
SCHOOLS, WORK, SPORTS EVENTS, RESTAURANTS

	Questions	Stars
Red Phase **STOP**	1. Did leaders stop and create urgency regarding the change?	
	2. Did people receive explanations of the change and when it was most likely to happen?	
	3. Were leaders leading an actionable response to the change?	
	4. Were those that were identified as being medium to highly impacted warned about the change coming? *This would include groups such as First Responders, The Elderly, Essential Workers, Transportation Industry and so on.*	
	5. Were the impacted groups informed how and why they were identified as moderate to highly impacted?	
	6. Were they told about the consequences of not changing?	
	7. Were they told about the rewards for changing?	
	8. Did those impacted express or feel confidence in their leaders?	
	Total # of Stars	**/8**

	Questions	Stars
Yellow Phase **PREPARE**	1. Did leaders start pandemic update meetings and communicate where they are in the process and where they want to be?	
	2. Were those impacted informed exactly what would change for them? *This would include new policies, rules, protocols, equipment, processes and so on.*	
	3. Were performance improvement measures identified? *E.g. Hospital capacity, required equipment and resources and so on.*	
	4.Were they told the skills needed and training(s) to complete? *E.g. Covid 19 testing, healthcare protocol training, prevention training and so on*	
	5.Were there incentive programs in identified? *These are rewards and consequences to help with a smooth translon of the change.*	
	6.Were barriers that might impact the change management identified, mitigated and communicated?	
	7. Did those that were impacted feel that the organization was ready for the change?	
	8. Did those impacted feel confident in their leader(s)?	
	Total # of Stars	**/8**

	Questions	Stars
Green Phase **ACT**	1. Did leaders continue pandemic update meetings and communicate where they are in the process and where they want to be?	
	2. Did leadership launch/begin the Change Management Strategy?	
	3. Were performance improvement measures implemented? *E.g. Enough hospital capacity, required equipment and resources.*	
	4. Were those impacted performing the required skills needed to help adapt to the change?	
	5. Were there incentive programs in place and working? *These are rewards and consequences to help adapt to the change.*	
	6. Were barriers that are impacting the change management being mitigated?	
	7. Did those that were impacted feel that the organization was handling the change appropriately?	
	8. Did those impacted feel confident in their leader(s)?	
	Total # of Stars	**/8**

What phase was your first phase that earned 4-Stars or fewer? _____

Here's my scoring for Example 2:

	Questions	Stars
Red Phase **STOP**	1. Did leaders stop and create urgency regarding the change?	*
	2. Did people receive explanations of the change and when it was most likely to happen?	*
	3. Were leaders leading an actionable response to the change?	*
	4.Were those that were identified as being medium to highly impacted warned about the change coming?	
	5.Were the impacted groups informed how and why they were identified as moderate to highly impacted?	*
	6.Were they told about the consequences of not changing?	*
	7. Were they told about the rewards for changing?	*
	8. Did those impacted express or feel confidence in their leaders?	
	Total # of Stars	**6/8**

Reasons for my **STOP** Phase scoring **6/8**:

- Leadership did an excellent job creating a sense of urgency and communicating the change they wanted.
- Leadership did an excellent job letting people know about the change: when, where, and why it would happen as well as to whom it would happen.

	Questions	Stars
Yellow Phase **PREPARE**	1. Did leaders start pandemic update meetings and communicate where they are in the process and where they want to be?	
	2. Were those impacted informed exactly what would change for them? *This would include new policies, rules, protocols, equipment, processes and so on.*	
	3. Were performance improvement measures identified? *E.g. Hospital capacity, required equipment and resources and so on.*	*
	4. Were they told the skills needed and training(s) to complete? *E.g. Covid 19 testing, healthcare protocol training, prevention training and so on*	
	5. Were there incentive programs in identified? *These are rewards and consequences to help with a smooth translon of the change.*	*
	6. Were barriers that might impact the change management identified, mitigated and communicated?	
	7. Did those that were impacted feel that the organization was ready for the change?	
	8. Did those impacted feel confident in their leader(s)?	
	Total # of Stars	**2/8**

	Questions	Stars
Green Phase **ACT**	1. Did leaders continue pandemic update meetings and communicate where they are in the process and where they want to be?	
	2. Did leadership launch/begin the Change Management Strategy?	
	3. Were performance improvement measures implemented? *E.g. Enough hospital capacity, required equipment and resources.*	
	4.Were those impacted performing the required skills needed to help adapt to the change?	
	5.Were there incentive programs in place and working? *These are rewards and consequences to help adapt to the change.*	
	6.Were barriers that are impacting the change management being mitigated?	
	7. Did those that were impacted feel that the organization was handling the change appropriately?	
	8. Did those impacted feel confident in their leader(s)?	
	Total # of Stars	**0/8**

Reasons for my scores given to the **Prepare (Yellow) and Act (Green)** Phases:

- There were reopening guidelines in place and communicated, but these were downplayed by President Trump.
- No proper plan was in place for enforcing the guidelines.
- No communication occurred on what would change for people specifically. It was simply business as usual.
- According to polls reported by PBS.org, most Americans did not feel ready or safe sending their kids to schools, going back to work, to sports events,

or to dine in restaurants. Most states had not met the experts' criteria for states to open.

- There were no performance improvement measures in place or enforced to support the change. E.g., Hospital capacity, enough resources and equipment, downward treads in cases.
- There was no communication on which trainings to complete. E.g., Healthcare guidelines, virus testing training, contact tracing, best practices, processes.
- They held no re-opening update meetings.
- No change management strategy was implemented. E.g. Communication plan, training programs.
- People did not receive the necessary supplies. E.g. virus test kits.
- An incentive program was not in place. Although rewards were naturally in place already. Most people wanted to open the economy. Paychecks, socializing, shopping are all rewards.

The **Yellow Phase (Prepare)** was the first phase that received 4-Stars or fewer. How do we address this stage, so it scores 5 stars or higher?

Once again, leadership needs to address our concerns and their answers must have actionable responses. For example, in preparation for the change, healthcare safety protocols would need to be in place for the score to increase to three or more stars. Some questions you may want to consider asking your leaders, including city officials, governors, mayors, senators, and presidents:

- When will we see business people and/or city employees being tested daily?
- What are the public protocols planned for containing this virus in the city? E.g., Disinfecting, public transportation, testing centers

- When will we see teachers and students being tested daily?
- When will it be mandatory for customers and employees to wear protective gear?
- How will the city protect the groups most infected (e.g., minorities)?
- How will the city or state enforce social distancing? E.g., Driving restrictions, restaurant protocols.

Let's look at one more example, but this time using a personal change you are experiencing. Write on a piece of paper a change that is happening to you or that you know will happen to you in the future. If you're the organization's leader, ask these questions (*Did I…*). If you are not the formal leader, ask yourself if your organization's leadership has addressed the following questions.

Rate each phase, using the star system as above.

EXAMPLE 3: YOUR PERSONAL CHANGE

	Questions	Stars
Red Phase **STOP**	1. Did leaders stop and create urgency regarding the change?	
	2. Did people receive explanations of the change and when it was most likely to happen?	
	3. Were leaders leading an actionable response to the change?	
	4. Were those that were identified as being medium to highly impacted warned about the change coming?	
	5. Were the impacted groups informed how and why they were identified as moderate to highly impacted?	
	6. Were they told about the consequences of not changing?	
	7. Were they told about the rewards for changing?	
	8. Did those impacted express or feel confidence in their leaders?	
	Total # of Stars	**/8**

	Questions	Stars
Yellow Phase **PREPARE**	1. Did leaders start change meetings and communicate where they are in the process and where they want to be?	
	2. Were those impacted informed exactly what would change for them?	
	3. Were performance improvement measures identified?.	
	4.Were they told the skills needed and training(s) to complete?	
	5.Were there incentive programs in identified?	
	6.Were barriers that might impact the change management identified, mitigated and communicated?	
	7. Did those that were impacted feel that the organization was ready for the change?	
	8. Did those impacted feel confident in their leader(s)?	
	Total # of Stars	**/8**

		Questions	Stars
Green Phase **ACT**		1. Did leaders continue pandemic update meetings and communicate where they are in the process and where they want to be?	
		2. Did leadership launch/begin the Change Management Strategy?	
		3. Were performance improvement measures implemented? *E.g. Enough hospital capacity, required equipment and resources.*	
		4.Were those impacted performing the required skills needed to help adapt to the change?	
		5.Were there incentive programs in place and working? *These are rewards and consequences to help adapt to the change.*	
		6.Were barriers that are impacting the change management being mitigated?	
		7. Did those that were impacted feel that the organization was handling the change appropriately?	
		8. Did those impacted feel confident in their leader(s)?	
		Total # of Stars	**/8**

What phase was your first score earning 4 stars or fewer?

_____

Depending on your phases(s) identified, there is a mitigation plan for each. You would start by addressing and communicating the unanswered questions. Note that these examples and exercises are only the tip of the iceberg on managing change, but they represent a required step. Holding leaders accountable to communicate their plans for the change is critically important and must happen. This is the key to a seamless, successful change in your organization. This is required for those leaders who are ignoring the change or who are not proactively managing it.

Experts around the world have warned us that the virus is not going away anytime soon, and it will have more waves as the months go on. These waves are changes that will disrupt our everyday lives. These will impact our bank accounts, our relationships, jobs, and, for many, deaths of our loved ones. The good news is that these are all changes we can help manage. These are all changes that we can plan for and advocate for their preparation. It would be heartbreaking if we did not learn from our past errors and our failures to act. We need to come together, to behave strategically, to make sure we do not make these same mistakes again.

CHAPTER XIV

The Sunny Side of 2020

The first four months of 2020 was a period of unique and dramatic change in our lives. It was a global event that we had only seen in movies or read in books. Organizations and individuals had to learn to adapt. Some organizations and individuals quicker than others, but nevertheless we adapted, and we will continue to adapt, readjust, and accommodate change until we find effective vaccines or treatments.

Just as in any organization, when a significant change happens, the culture of the company or organization changes. During all of this, it's easy to feel that negative outcomes outnumber positive ones. But, despite difficulties imposed by change, positive variables, too, can come to light – indeed, they almost always do. In the case of the current pandemic, several favorable outcomes have become obvious, at least in the short term. We have yet to see what the future brings. Here are some positive outcomes due to the pandemic so far.

SCIENTIST and TECHNOLOGIES

The seemingly fastest ever collaboration between technology and scientist is happening because of this virus.

Scientists around the world have united to focus on one problem, finding a vaccine. We're seeing the sharing of real-time information and the use of new (as well as proven) technologies. We see this with testing. As soon as China declared an epidemic outbreak, they shared the virus's genome sequence immediately. This would allow global testing to begin, even though tests had not yet been perfected. To date, testing improvements are still being made, and we continue to benefit from the scientific community's cooperative efforts to share information quickly and without prejudice.

Also, there's IBM's Summit supercomputer, the world's fastest. Pressured by the ever-growing pandemic, researchers, by the end of April, were running thousands of simulations via the computer; at that point, it had found 77 drug compounds that might potentially become part of a vaccine. It's hard to estimate how much longer this process would have taken to yield the information we have up to this point, without the urgency imposed by the pandemic and its devastating effects.

Researchers are also investigating repurposing medications that currently are used to treat other diseases. The rationale is that this process is likely to be more efficient, finding new therapeutic applications for an existing drug than having to create a new one. One example is Remdesivir, which has already shown promise in clinical trials involving 70 patients. Results of one study showed that Remdesivir inhibits virus effects by blocking an enzyme that the virus uses, thus shortening recovery time for patients. Other pharmaceuticals currently being tested include Favilavir, Ivermectin, and Chloroquine.

There is reason to hope. Effective vaccines and pharmaceutical therapies will be discovered for this virus. Recall how lethal bacterial infections used to be, killing hundreds of thousands of people, before penicillin came on the scene? And polio; at one time, poliomyelitis was rampant around the world, but now, due to vaccines directed at this disease, it is far less common (although not non-existent). HIV still does not have a vaccine and annual deaths attributable to this disease are staggeringly high in some parts of the world. But there *are* HIV-targeted treatments, allowing many people to live a fuller life than would have been possible otherwise. So, let's remind ourselves: Times are tough right now, but a pandemic has never beaten us in the history of humanity, and this pandemic won't either.

CLIMATE IS IMPROVING

With transportation needs curtailed, at least temporarily, reductions in the use of gas-fueled vehicles (e.g., cars, airplanes) have resulted in the lowest levels of CO_2 emissions since the financial crisis over a decade ago. On March 19, the BBC reported that levels of air pollutants and warming gases over some cities and regions had already shown significant drops. Also, researchers in New York told the BBC that early results showed carbon monoxide emissions, mainly from cars, had reduced by nearly 50% compared with the previous year. The emission of the planet-heating gas CO_2 had fallen sharply as well.

Hypergiant, a technology company based in Austin, Texas, is using Artificial Intelligence to show the impact of the pandemic on climate change. They report that the US is on track for a 7% decrease in annual emission, the greatest reduction in the country's history. Hypergiant CEO Ben Lamm explains their AI product: "The tool was created to put widely circulated reports of pandemic-related emissions reductions in the context of fundamental climate science…We can't ignore the next crisis because of the one we are currently fighting."

CAR LANES TO BIKE LANES

Image 27. Bike lanes

More and more cities around the world have been converting car lanes into bike lanes, prompted initially by concerns to alleviate transmission of the virus. This is almost certainly why restrictions were put on public transportation, at least in the short-term, to halt the spread by eliminating great numbers of people in close quarters on buses, subways, and the like. But it turns out that doing so provided the valuable benefit of improved air quality. Paris is an exemplar in having the foresight to create many new bike lanes that encouraged people to venture out of their homes again, to move around the city, to maintain healthy habits, and to help restart the economy. According to the Wall Street Journal, Paris is making 50 km of lanes formerly used by cars into bike-only thoroughfares and another 30 streets will be pedestrian-only. The idea has caught ahold, with more and more car-to-bike lane conversions happening in the suburbs of Paris.

This trend in Paris can be seen in the US as well. *The Guardian* reports that Philadelphia converted 4.7 miles of roadway into bike lanes. Minneapolis closed part of their riverfront for bikes. Oakland is planning to convert 74 miles of roads, 10% of its total. Many other cities around the world are following suit, including Vancouver, Budapest, Sydney,

Chapel Hill, Calgary, Berlin, Bogota, Mexico City, and London. It's a great trend that we hope continues.

LESS VIOLENCE

According to CBS News, Miami went seven weeks without a homicide for the first time since 1957. The *New York Times* reported that in Chicago, one of America's most violent cities, drug arrests have plummeted 42% in the weeks since the city shut down, compared with the same period last year. The *Times* also reported that, across Latin America, crime is down to levels unseen in decades. El Salvador reported an average of two killings a day in March, down from a peak of 600 per day a few years ago. Here in Costa Rica, *La Nacion* (newspaper) also reported a reduction in organized crime and homicides.

COSTA RICA OPENS NATIONAL TOURISIM

Because of Costa Rica's change management of the outbreak, the country was on a downward trajectory of cases. Although it had never closed the economy entirely, the government had initially put many restrictions in place. After weeks of such belt-tightening across the country, officials now felt it was safe to open beaches and national tourism in Costa Rica. They were carefully monitoring how people were behaving, whether rules were being followed. Beaches, for example, were open for only three hours a day and only during the workweek, not on weekends. Some other changes: parks opened at 50% capacity, only non-contact sports could be played, restaurant opened at 50% capacity, hotels 50% (maximum of 20 rooms). The Minister of Health explained the conditions: if social distancing was being followed, in June more liberties would be considered that would help our economy. These included welcoming small cruise ships and flights into the country. He also explained how dine-in restaurants would work, with "group bubbles" (each table group separated by 2 meters from the next table) helping people achieve appropriate social distancing.

ORGANIZATIONS ADAPT QUICKLY

We began to see many proactive examples of Change Management in action, in organizations such as banks, restaurants, grocery stores, and many more; these were system prototypes preparing for the new normal. What was fascinating to me is how quickly they were making these needed adaptations. This illustrates perfectly that, if rewards or consequences are strong enough, change can happen quickly. By contrast, if the reward or consequence doesn't have an immediate impact, change can be similarly slow to occur.

For example, one day a scientist somewhere proved that secondhand cigarette smoke was damaging to others. Up until then, smoking was allowed in bars, airports, airplanes, restaurants, everywhere. What some people may have thought of as their God-given "freedom" was now proven to hurt others. Change from a smoking culture to one that decried it was not fast; in fact, it took years for smoking laws to pass. This change was also imperfect; it was trial and error. For example, initial laws didn't completely ban smoking. Instead, zones were created for "smoking" and "non-smoking" sections in public places. Often, smoking sections were situated right next to non-smoking sections, with nothing to prevent smoke from traveling to the area where it was prohibited. Not very helpful, right?

Some improvements were made, but change was still not perfect. Smoking was restricted in most restaurants, but you could still smoke in bars and clubs. A few years later, laws were enacted that restricted smoking in all public places. Nowadays, this feels normal. But why did it take so long, with so many change management iterations that failed to hit the desired mark? I believe this change took longer to occur globally because consequences (at least the negative ones) were not immediate enough to lead to behavioral and legislative change. That is, lung problems related to secondhand smoke was a too-distant outcome for most people to care about or to see as a real threat. Short-term pleasure outweighed long-term health habits. However, slowly, with complaints by non-smokers, and scientifically proven cases that underscored the risk, laws passed and people began to change. This virus has a more immediate consequence, so hopefully we will continue to see more rapid changes in response to this crisis.

GOOD NEWS IN THE ANIMAL WORLD

Animals are also enjoying the new normal. Several amazing videos came out, showing wildlife being themselves in nature, freed from interference by humans and human activities. Creatures of all sorts were finally feeling comfortable in their own home. We saw goats enjoying city streets in Wales, wild pigs crossing streets in Israel, jellyfish in the canals of Venice, and, my personal favorite, a puma caught on a security camera strolling around the streets of my hometown, Heredia, Costa Rica.

Image 28. Puma roaming town in Costa Rica

PRESIDENTIAL LEADERS BEATING THE VIRUS

I was pleased that, in only four months, many presidential leaders were beating the virus. There are many that did an outstanding job, some honorable mentions: Uruguay, Belize, Iceland, Thailand, and Ireland. But these are not the only exemplars. I would also like to acknowledge all those at the local, state, and provincial levels around the world who have led the change responsibly, especially in countries saddled with poor leadership at the top. We've been lucky to have people in positions of power who were early adapters and who continued to guide their countries throughout the change to the point that disruptions were minimal. These people are genuine leaders that the world can learn from as we move forward out of this crisis. Here are four models:

The President of Vietnam, Nguyen Phu Trong, and his advisors have shown great leadership throughout the pandemic. **As of May 1st , Vietnam had a rate of 0.27 cases per 100,000 people and 0 deaths**.

Image 29 President Nguyen Phu Trong

According to the latest polling data from YouGov.com, Vietnam was leading the list of countries most supportive of government efforts to combat the virus. Nearly all (95%) Vietnamese people feel that their government is handling the crisis "very" or "somewhat well." According to another poll by the same company, Vietnam also rated very high in their fear of the virus, with 89% of the Vietnam population stating they were "very" or "somewhat" concerned they will contract the disease. However, according to Forbes magazine, a new working paper from the University of Tokyo in Japan, explained why the virus fear and effective crisis management might not coincide. The study surveyed 2,800 Japanese adults, the research found that even non-mandatory government protocols were effective in increasing caution. In other words, in times of pandemic, a government's ability to instill a healthy, not over the top or militant amount of fear in its citizens may be one of the more effective ways to keep them healthy.

I do not find this surprising because I experienced the same thing here in Costa Rica. The urgency and appropriate amount of fear/caution of the pandemic, instilled by credible leaders and scientists, motivated me to listen, ask questions, and to change without being forced to do so.

Another prominent leader who was an early adapter to the pandemic is the President of Taiwan, Tsai Ing-wen, as well as her advisors. **On May 1st , Taiwan reported a rate of 1.75 cases per 100,000 people and only 6 deaths.**

Image 30 President Tsai Ing-wen

The fear of being next door to the epicenter (at the time) could be the principal reason, at least initially, that Taiwan's pandemic management performance was so impressive. However, the *Journal of the American Medical Association* states that Taiwan engaged in 124 discrete interventions to prevent the spread of the disease, including early communication and training regarding the interventions, such as screening of flights from mainland China and tracking individual cases. This is Change Management at its finest, and it did not go unnoticed. Taiwan received international praise, especially for the effectiveness in quarantining with the use of an electronic fence system to slow down the spread of the virus.

An electronic fence is a system to monitor phone signals to alert police and local officials if those in-home quarantines move away from their address or turn off their phones. Taiwan had been in front of their testing; by mid-May they had completed 69,000 tests.

On a smaller population scale, three exemplary leaders come to mind, one of which is the Prime Minister of Finland, Sanna Mirella Marin, and her advisors. **On May 1st, Finland showed a rate of 90.9 cases per 100,000 people and 218 deaths.**

Image 31 Prime Minister Marin and European Council
Charles Miche

Although these numbers seem high, we should remember that Finland borders Sweden, which had no pandemic restrictions enforced in their country. Finland reacted quickly. On March 16, they implemented the Emergency Powers Act, to be in place until April 13 (later extended to May 13). This was a lockdown act for the country. Here are a few restrictions of that act, according to Helsinki Times:

- All schools will be closed, including early education.
- Most government-run public facilities (theatres, libraries, museums, etc.) will be shut down.

- At most 10 people can participate in a public meeting, and people over the age of 70 should avoid human contact if possible.
- Outsiders are forbidden from entering healthcare facilities and hospitals, excluding relatives of critically ill people and children.
- The capacity of social and healthcare will be increased in the private and public sector, while less critical activity will be decreased.
- Preparations for the shutdown of borders will start, and citizens or permanent residents returning to Finland will be placed under a 2-week quarantine.

Another early adapter is the President of Costa Rica, Carlos Alvarado Quesada, and his advisors. **On May 1st, Costa Rica had a rate of 14.3 cases per 100,000 people and 6 deaths.**

Image 32 President of Costa Rica Carlos Alvarado

Starting early in the pandemic and continuing throughout the quarter, President Alvarado has shown strong leadership. Almost immediately, he facilitated the needs of the Ministry of Health. He let the scientific experts take charge of pandemic management. He listened to precautions they advised him to take for the country. He then supported them and expedited their recommendations, so that needs were addressed as quickly as possible. Humility is a sign of a great leader and President Alvarado showed it. His competent, confident, and courageous leadership undoubtedly saved thousands of lives. Moreover, it allowed Costa Rica to avoid entirely closing its economy and to open up sooner with better social safety habits firmly in place. It also bought us time for the scientific research community to find a vaccine.

The Prime Minister of New Zealand, Jacinda Ardern, and her advisors were also exceptional. **On April 30, New Zealand had a rate of 29.5 cases per 100,000 people and 6 deaths.**

Image 33 President Jacinda Ardern

To manage the outbreak, Ardern and her government implemented a four alert level system on March 21, exemplifying the kind of out-of-the-gate leadership that is needed to put effective, early change management in place. The alert level was initially set at level 2 but was subsequently raised to level 3 on March 23. By March 25, the alert level was at 4, putting the country into a nationwide lockdown. New Zealand's alert level eventually decreased from 4 to level 2. In fact, on some days there were no reported cases. By mid-May, lockdown restrictions were lifted, while physical distancing was maintained. Through these strong initial efforts, on-going evaluation and re-evaluation of conditions, and follow through, New Zealand became a genuine success story on how to cope with and defeat the pandemic.

These countries, as well as others, should be studied from a performance improvement perspective. They have protocols, communication strategies, trainings, technologies, and other solutions that can benefit us all. These solutions can help the world defeat this virus now but, as well, they can help us deal with pandemics that are sure to come in the future.

CHAPTER XV

What Have We Learned So Far?

From January through April 2020, Costa Rica implemented 10 performance improvement interventions that allowed it to successfully manage the pandemic:

1. SECURE AIRPORTS: Test symptoms before allowing travelers to enter the country (before the outbreak).
2. LISTEN TO EXPERTS: Let experts lead the pandemic response, with Presidential support to facilitate recommendations.
3. CONTROL CROWDS: Control mass gatherings.
4. ALTER SHOPPING: Limit essential goods per person and implement store safety measures.
5. ACTIVATE LOCAL LEADERSHIP: Update all communications and enforce protocols.
6. IMPLEMENT DRIVING RESTRICTIONS: Restrict driving hours to reduce virus mobility.
7. CONTROL BORDERS: Test and control number of people coming in through all points of entry.
8. INFORM CHILDREN: Children deserve information. They need to know what is happening, in words they

can understand. They are social creatures who can easily spread germs, so it's critical that they understand, and participate in, the new normal.

9. OPEN ECONOMY WITH PROTOCOLS: This should occur slowly and only when there's a downward trajectory of new cases and deaths. This is especially crucial at the beginning of the pandemic.

10. ACTIVATE TESTING and CONTACT TRACING: Testing and contact tracing is essential but must be efficient. Testing should include targeting wastewater in potential hot-spot communities and monitoring for other related viruses and bacteria, such as influenza and diarrhea.

This change, the pandemic, came upon us quickly. We know that, even as we progress through it, the pandemic and the challenges it presents can all change in an instant, for the worse or the better. We have learned that we are not invincible (indeed, we never are), and it has become clear to us that nothing stays the same, not even our lifestyles. But we have also learned that we can come together during difficult times. I'm grateful to have been alive to experience this period in history, because I've been able to observe the strength and resilience of my fellow humans and I appreciate it more than ever before.

Worldwide, we see the power of germs, viruses, and the like and understand, perhaps more clearly than ever before, the real threat they can be to society and to the world's economies. I feel there is a newfound respect for scientists, specifically epidemiologists, as they are the leaders that guide us during virus outbreaks.

We know that this story is far from over and that we must change the way we live in order to adapt. People are calling this time "the new normal." Many outcomes are possible. It could be that more countries decide to take a herd immunity approach, possibly at the expense of human health. If so, I hope these countries have a well-established healthcare system to support this approach. We also may see more countries periodically flattening the curve and taking calculated risks in order to open parts of their economies.

Lastly, I feel we have learned that not creating urgency, and downplaying or trivializing a pandemic, only leads to more deaths, and does so without escaping economic instability. There's no getting around it; a pandemic will, indeed, strain economies. But it will also strain human survival. So, the balance between economy and health should never initially favor the economy. Ensuring the health of all the world's citizens must be addressed as a fundamental priority and science must be allowed to guide first-response plans to contain outbreaks. Economic priorities should not win the day, at least not the first ones, weeks or months.

Many countries have unfortunately taught us this. We now know that there is a way to handle a pandemic that protects both human life and the economy, and the winning strategy is to put these priorities in the right order. As of May 1, here are the top 4 countries with the most cases and deaths at the time.

Country	Rate of Cases per 100,000	Deaths
USA	346.1	67,044
Italy	343.8	28,177
Spain	513.3	24,824
UK	236.1	27,510

CHAPTER XVI

...And Then We Change

There will be countless changes in the world because of the pandemic. More waves will come, bringing unemployment, protests, conspiracy theories, fake news, and much more. These changes may or may not be logical, scientific, safe, or necessary. Regardless, we need to get in front of these challenges, finding out all we can, in order to respond effectively. This book has presented a Change Management technique, *Stop, Prepare, Act,* showing us how to mitigate changes that we face. Using *Stop, Prepare, Act* to reduce negative impacts can make adapting to these changes less difficult.

As a leader, creating *urgency* is imperative. This means communicating the coming change to your organization as soon as possible, regardless if you agree with it or not. So, how can you do that? Communicate to your family, work, school, town, state, country, wherever you have influence. Identify the pros and cons for you or your organization. What will happen if you don't change? What will happen if you do change? What are the consequences or rewards? Maybe you're reluctant to support the change; even so, you will still have to help others prepare and adapt so that there is minimal impact on your organization as a whole. This means finding out precisely what you will need to do to ensure a smooth response overall. You can find out more details regarding the upcoming change, possibly requiring more communication, decisions, tools, supplies, or resources. Will you or your organization need training, or do they already know how to adapt to the change? How can the change be reinforced, so that it becomes the norm? Finding these answers will put you and your organization in a position of power in mitigating the change.

Without a doubt, there will be organizations such as states, cities, schools, gyms, bars, and restaurants having very few or no protocols. But, there will be others, organizations with protocols firmly in place, braced for change and ready for the challenges ahead. I can already see these smart organizations applying their protocols, practicing *Stop, Prepare, Act.* Imagine a restaurant that communicates their house rules on a huge board:

1. *We follow healthcare protocols to keep our restaurant and economy open.* (Stop) They are creating urgency.
2. *Mandatory two-meter distance between social bubbles. Masks MUST be used at all times when not at your table.* (Stop) They are communicating the "change" for the customer.
3. *A free pitcher of beer or dessert for social bubbles that follow the bar rules without requiring warnings.* (Prepare) They are communicating what is in it for you and preparing you for the change.
4. *Pitchers are of domestic beers only, or 1 dessert per social bubble.* (Prepare) They are communicating more specific details about the change.
5. *If you do not know how to use a mask, no worries, our waiters are trained to show you how to use one properly.* (Act) They are communicating and

providing training for the action/change that is required.

6. *Warning! We have a "3 strikes, you are out" policy. If we warn you 3x to put your mask on, we will ask you to pay your bill and leave.* (Act) They have an incentive policy in place to assure the change is consistent once it's being performed.

The Change Management technique of *Stop, Prepare, Act* is powerful and empowering. It can be used for any challenges that you are experiencing now or that you will experience in the future. It's equally applicable in your personal life and in your work world. It's up to you to decide if and how you want to respond, when fate throws you a curve. Smart leadership is at a premium. We can be part of it. Remember, we are all in this together, so let's be kind with each other as we change our world.

If you are interested in learning more about Change Management, Performance Improvement or would like 1:1 coaching or consultation, please contact me at ppc.esch@gmail.com or go to our website www.proactiveperformanceconsulting.com and receive a 50% discount on one of our workshops.

THANK YOU

I would like to thank you for taking the time to read my book. I appreciate you very much. **Amazon.com and Goodread.com reviews are extremely important for authors.** Please leave a review so that others can be exposed to the book. Also, don't forget to share your review on social media with hashtag #BrightLightDarkPandemic.
Stay Healthy

Acknowledgments

Writing this book *about* the pandemic, *during* the pandemic, has been an unexpected gift to me. It turned out to be therapeutic for me in these difficult times. But I recognize that I couldn't have done this alone. I'd like to thank my amazing beta readers and editors. First, Marilyn Alan who went above and beyond what I expected. You really made a big difference for the betterment of the book and I thank you so much for your feedback. I also want to thank my dear stepmother, also a beta reader and editor who supported me from the beginning, and I am not only talking about from the beginning of this book, but also my life. Your advice is always valuable and your editing skills are incredible. To my lovely mother for your unconditional love and brining me to this world and inspiring me to write and to express myself. To my dad, for teaching me to finish what I start, and for making sure I do not neglect my health. To my sister, for helping me brainstorm through a writing block and for your support. Thank you to my wonderful girlfriend, who has experienced my difficulties in writing this book and has put up with me throughout the entire process. Thank you, love, for your patience and support. To my niece and nephew and rest of my family for being so sweet and supportive. To my best friend, Rafie, for his unconditional canine love and needs, forcing me to leave my computer and get some fresh air! Finally, to you, my readers including those that endorsed my book, I appreciate you more than you know and I hope to keep publishing interesting and useful books for you. Until next time.

About the Author

For the last 20+ years, Alejandro has been focusing on areas such as Performance Improvement, Coaching, Team Building, Instructional Systems Design and Change Management. He has worked in several industries and organization a crossed the world.

In the US he has worked and lived in California, Michigan, Florida, Illinois, Indiana, and Texas. He also lived and worked in Argentina, Costa Rica, Venezuela, Holland, India and England. He has a passion for people and cultures around the world. It is for this reason Alejandro has dedicated his professional life to Change Management and Performance Improvement in organizations. His Consulting business, Proactive Performance Consulting works with systematic approaches that are fun, interactive and effective in improving human and organizational performance. He is fully dedicated to sharing and exchanging experiences, knowledge & tools to as many people and organizations as possible.

CONNECT WITH ALEJANDRO ON:
Email: ppc.esch@gmail.com
Website: www.Proactiveperformanceconsulting.com
Linkedin:www.linkedin.com/in/proactiveperformanceconsulting/
Twiter: @ProactivePerfo1

Index

References

Image 1. Prime Minister of New Zealand
Retrieved 4/20/2020
Wikimedia Commons
https://commons.wikimedia.org/wiki/Main_Page
By Governor-General of New Zealand - Appointment of the new
Ministry, CC BY 4.0,
https://commons.wikimedia.org/w/index.php?curid=63669064

Image 2. Chancellor of Germany and President of Norway
Retrieved 4/20/2020
Wikimedia Commons
https://commons.wikimedia.org/wiki/Main_Page
By FinnishGovernment - Pääministeri Marin Berliinissä
19.2.2020, CC BY 2.0,
https://commons.wikimedia.org/w/index.php?curid=89376386

Image 3. President of Taiwan
Retrieved 4/20/2020
Wikimedia Commons
https://commons.wikimedia.org/wiki/Main_Page
By Office of the President - Flickr, CC BY 2.0,
https://commons.wikimedia.org/w/index.php?curid=88888990

Image 4. Dr. Li Wenliang
Retrieved 4/20/2020
Wikimedia Commons
https://commons.wikimedia.org/wiki/Main_Page
By Par PetrVod — Travail personnel, CC BY-SA 4.0,
https://commons.wikimedia.org/w/index.php?curid=89424178

Image 5. Dr. Daniel Salas
Retrieved 4/20/2020
Wikimedia Commons
https://commons.wikimedia.org/wiki/Main_Page
Csavil / CC BY-SA
(https://creativecommons.org/licenses/by-sa/4.0)

Image 6. Italian Flag
Retrieved 4/20/2020
Wikimedia Commons
https://commons.wikimedia.org/wiki/Main_Page
De Pietro Luca Cassarino -
https://www.flickr.com/photos/184568471@N07/49689932383/, CC
BY-SA 4.0,
https://commons.wikimedia.org/w/index.php?curid=88461537

Image 7. Albanians Doctors helping Italy
Retrieved 4/20/2020
Wikimedia Commons
https://commons.wikimedia.org/wiki/Main_Page
By Dipartimento Protezione Civile - Dipartimento Protezione Civile,
CC BY 2.0,
https://commons.wikimedia.org/w/index.php?curid=89384780

Image 8. Rescue Medical Ship in NYC bay.
Retrieved 4/20/2020
Wikimedia Commons
https://commons.wikimedia.org/wiki/Main_Page
By MusikAnimal - Own work, CC BY-SA 4.0,
https://commons.wikimedia.org/w/index.php?curid=88769235

Image 9. Surfer running from police
Retrieved 4/20/2020
Instagram https://www.instagram.com/
By Surfline
https://www.instagram.com/p/BTHoy1Hwd_/?utm_source=ig_embe
d
Image 10. National Pandemic Situation
Retrieved 4/20/2020
Ministerio de Salud Costa Rica www.ministeriodesalud.go.cr
Daily Dashboard
https://www.ministeriodesalud.go.cr/index.php/centro-de-
prensa/noticias/741-noticias-2020/1725-situacion-nacional-covid-19

Image 11. Daniel Ortega
Retrieved 4/20/2020
Wikipedia https://en.wikipedia.org/wiki/Main_Page
By Fundación Ong DE Nicaragua - Own work, CC BY-SA 3.0,
https://commons.wikimedia.org/w/index.php?curid=20349494

Image 12. of Makeshift Costa Airport on boarder
Retrieved 4/20/2020
CrHoy www.crhoy.com
By CrHoy
https://www.crhoy.com/mundo/video-asi-castigan-en-panama-a-
quienes-violan-la-cuarentena-por-covid-19/

Image 13. Panamanians Community Service
Retrieved 4/20/2020
CrHoy www.crhoy.com
By CrHoy
https://www.crhoy.com/mundo/video-asi-castigan-en-panama-a-
quienes-violan-la-cuarentena-por-covid-19/

Image 14. Pandemic Children's book
Retrieved 4/20/2020
Unicef https://www.unicef.org/
Autor
Pixelatl con OPS, ONU, PNUD, UNICEF, OMS
https://www.unicef.org/costarica/informes/los-dias-que-todo-se-
detuvo

Image 16. National Free Healthcare Center
Retrieved 4/20/2020
El Observador, www.observador.cr
By El Observador
https://observador.cr/noticia/temor-ansiedad-y-atencion-adaptada-la-
vida-en-la-primera-linea-de-combate-del-coronavirus/

Image 17. Francisco Munguia Art
Retrieved 4/20/2020
La Nación www.lanacion.com
By Francisco Munguía
https://www.nacion.com/viva/cultura/fallece-el-artista-francisco-
munguia-el-
muralista/ASYIJHGMGRBT5MVRNDJPINHU44/story/

Image 18. Plasma Serum Process
Retrieved 4/20/2020
UCR www.ucr.com
By UCR and Instituto Clodomiro Picado
https://www.ucr.ac.cr/noticias/2020/04/27/asi-avanza-el-instituto-
clodomiro-picado-de-la-ucr-para-elaborar-el-suero-contra-el-covid-
19.html

Image 19. Supplies from China
Retrieved 4/20/2020
La Nación www.lanacion.com
By La Nación
https://www.nacion.com/el-pais/salud/llego-a-costa-rica-avion-con-
donacion-de-china/GBYCHI3PMJBCFBQOK6SO5IRFPY/story/

Image 20. Pope Francis
Retrieved 4/20/2020
By La Cancellara de Ecuador
https://www.flickr.com/people/10021639@N05 - This file has been
extracted from another file: FRANCISCOECUADOR.png, CC BY-
SA 2.0,
https://commons.wikimedia.org/w/index.php?curid=59877855

Image 21. Protocolos for entering house

Retrieved 4/20/2020
Periodicodeibiza.es
Protocolos de Salida, Entrada
https://www.periodicodeibiza.es/pitiusas/ibiza/2020/03/19/1149933/
protocolos-salida-entrada-casa-como-convivir-personas-riesgo-del-
covid-19.html

Image 22. Andrew Cuomo
Retrieved 4/20/2020
Wikipedia https://en.wikipedia.org/wiki/Main_Page
By Metropolitan Transportation Authority / Patrick Cashin -
https://www.flickr.com/photos/mtaphotos/31192356394/, CC BY
2.0,
https://commons.wikimedia.org/w/index.php?curid=59179257

Image 23. Refrigerated containers for the dead in NYC
Retrieved 4/20/2020
By Archer West - The uploader on Wikimedia Commons received
this from the author/copyright holder., CC BY 4.0,
https://commons.wikimedia.org/w/index.php?curid=89477234

Image 24. Dr. Asking protestors to let ambulance through
Retrieved 4/20/2020
Detroit News, www.detroitnews.com
By Detroit News
https://www.detroitnews.com/story/news/local/michigan/2020/04/16
/lansing-hospital-protest-caused-delays-shift-change/5144812002/

Image 25 Dr. Fauci
Retrieved 4/20/2020
By NIAID - Anthony S. Fauci, M.D., NIAID Director, CC BY 2.0,
https://commons.wikimedia.org/w/index.php?curid=82983928

Image 26 Dr. Fauci in White House
Retrieved 4/20/2020
By The White House -
https://www.flickr.com/photos/whitehouse/49723232743/, Public
Domain,
https://commons.wikimedia.org/w/index.php?curid=88827557

Image 27. Dead person left on street in Ecuador
Retrieved 4/20/2020
Punto de Corte, www.putodecorte.com

By Punto de corte-
https://puntodecorte.com/guayas-es-la-region-mas-afectada-por-covid-19-en-ecuador/

Image 28. Campaign to keep the elderly safe
Retrieved 4/20/2020
El Observador, www.elobservador.com
By El Observador
https://observador.cr/noticia/mas-de-la-mitad-de-adultos-mayores-que-contrajeron-covid-19-en-el-pais-lo-vencieron-y-ya-estan-recuperados/

Image 29. Bike lanes
Retrieved 4/20/2020
Good News Network, www.goodnewsnetwork.org
By Good News Network
https://www.goodnewsnetwork.org/page/47/?option=com_content&task=view&id=736&Itemid=0

Image 30. Puma roaming town in Costa Rica
Retrieved 4/20/2020
www.semanariouniversidad.com/
Semanario Universidad
https://semanariouniversidad.com/pais/camara-de-seguridad-capta-a-un-puma-caminando-por-calle-herediana/

Image 31 President Nguyen Phu Trong
Retrieved 4/20/2020
By Presidential Communications Operations Office - Presidential Communications Operations Office (Immediate: [1]), Public Domain,
https://commons.wikimedia.org/w/index.php?curid=73445913

Image 32 President Tsai Ing-wen
Retrieved 4/20/2020
By Wang Yu Ching / Office of the President -
https://www.flickr.com/photos/presidentialoffice/48131438417/, CC BY 2.0,
https://commons.wikimedia.org/w/index.php?curid=80020614

Image 33 Prime Minister Marin and European Council Charles Miche

141

"Change management has been a practice in business for decades. And yet all too often, major transformational projects still fail to manage the change effectively. The author introduces a simple, yet effective change management framework as demonstrated using traffic light signals: red, yellow, and green. In each step, critical questions must be answered in order to proceed to the next step. Skipping steps does not work. Esch puts this model to the test with the greatest transformation the world is facing in the 21st century, the pandemic of Covid-19. Anyone active in their local society probably has an opinion on how their local government has handled the pandemic. Esch outlines key data points on the pandemic timeline and applies the change model in **Bright Light Dark Pandemic**. Marrying the data to the model painfully reveals how poorly and how well some leaders handled the crisis, ultimately impacting the virus spread and human deaths. Whether you are in business or a community leader, you'll appreciate Esch's personal storytelling of his pandemic experience in his current home country, Costa Rica and his practical application to a powerful change management model."
---Jocelyn Chan, Enterprise Learning Director, AECOM

"In the early months of 2020, the world came to a screeching halt. A small but powerful virus overwhelmed the world forcing everyone to react to the pandemic. Using a real life crisis, the author skillfully weaves in the principles of change management and examines the, oh so different, responses of various governments, including his native Costa Rica and his second home country of the United States. The book offers a great juxtaposition of how Costa Rica and the United States have handled the pandemics. While Costa Rican leaders, with Dr. Salas at the forefront, were telling people to stay home, in the U.S., the Trump administration was still calling the virus a hoax and claiming to have everything under control.

The author, with a journalistic precision documents the events surrounding the COVID-19 outbreak worldwide. However, it is the very personal notes sprinkled throughout the book that make the story so relatable and relevant. We all felt what the author felt: fear of the unknown, fear for our loved ones, uncertainty and angst.

In his book, Esch, an experienced change management champion, offers tools to manage a crisis. He reaches to his consulting playbook and offers a solution to managing a change of any proportions. It is as simple as Stop. Prepare. Act.

The story goes from dark to bright and leaves the reader with an optimistic message: the ability of organizations and individuals to adapt to a "new normal" is powerful and that we can only emerge stronger from a crisis.

--- Edyta Zydorek, International Counsel at NCH

Made in the USA
Columbia, SC
09 November 2020